古蜀文化三星堆

Sanxingdui and the Ancient Shu Culture

中国旅游出版社
China Travel & Tourism Press

蹈循历史印迹

FOLLOWING THE PRINTS OF HISTORY AND TASTING THE SWEET DEW OF CIVILIZATION

品味文明甘霖

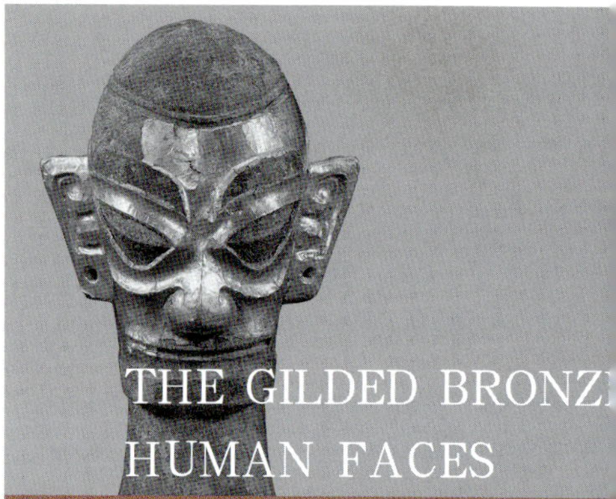

10 三星堆博物馆
SANXINGDUI MUSEUM

20 三星堆青铜人像群
BRONZE HUMAN FIGURES

48 三星堆青铜金面像
THE GILDED BRONZE HUMAN FACES

BRONZE OBJECTS
三星堆青铜器
54

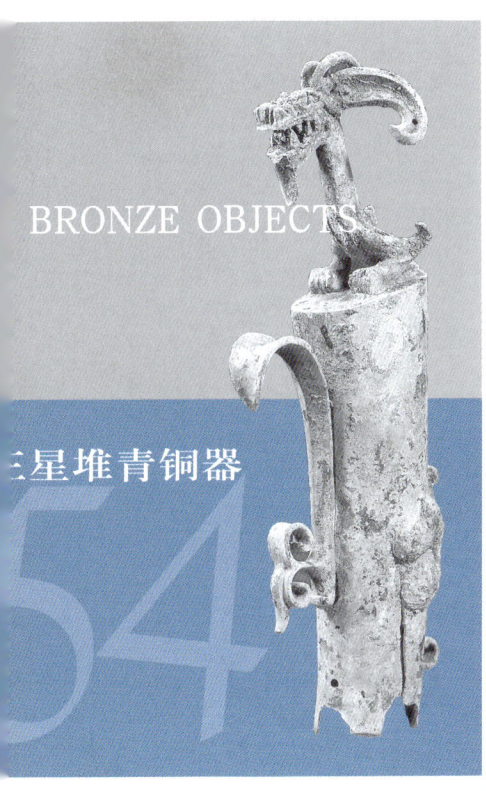

三星堆玉石器
80

JADE AND STONE OBJECTS

GRAY POTTERY
三星堆灰陶
88

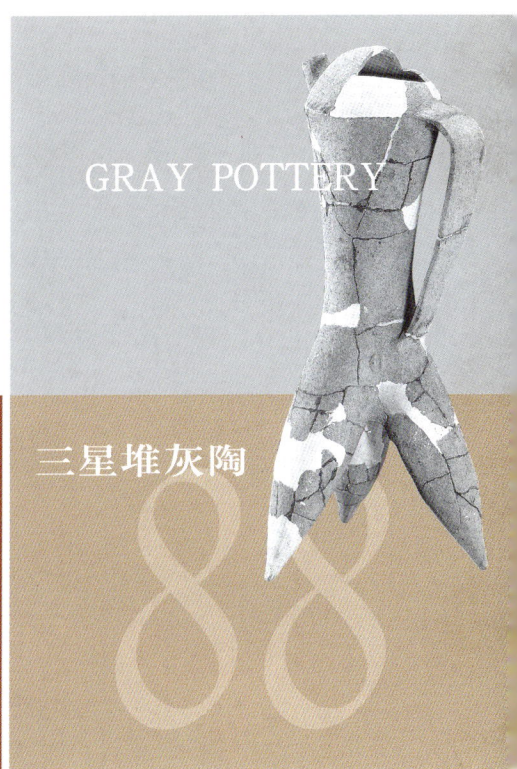

三星堆遗址在四川省的位置图
Location of the Ruins at Sanxingdui in Sichuan Province

前　言

　　唐代大诗人李白在《蜀道难》一诗中吟唱道："蚕丛及鱼凫，开国何茫然！尔来四万八千岁，不与秦塞通人烟"。此诗句虽然有些夸张，但亦可窥见传说中蜀人历史的渺茫与久远。要想探索蜀人的起源，实在是难于上青天。然而，悠久历史的必然辉煌，又存在于偶然的瞬间发现。1929年，四川广汉南兴镇月亮湾(今真武村)燕氏农民祖孙三人在掏车水坑、准备安放水车时，偶然发现了一堆色彩斑斓的玉石，共清理出璧、璋、琮、珠、玉料等珍贵文物400余件。一扇古蜀历史文化的大门因之而悄然洞开，沉睡了数千年的古蜀王国如梦初醒。

　　1933年冬至1934年春，华西大学博物馆(今四川大学博物馆)的美籍教授葛维汉以及林名均教授带领考古队进驻月亮湾，取得了大量的考古资料和实物标本。在以后的几十年里，几代考古学者相继在此考古发掘，取得了重大成果。东、西、南三面城墙的确认，使古城遗址呈现在眼前。总面积2.6平方公里，与郑州商城相当，是当时全国五大商城之一。大型宫殿遗址的发掘清理，以及数以万件文物的出土，硕果累累，引人瞩目。其中的鸟首陶勺柄，其绝对年代距今4000年到2500年之间。所谓鸟首图案，就是被艺术化了的鸬鹚，俗称鱼老鸦，即鱼凫。它以图腾形式代表了鱼凫族，象征了古蜀王国的鱼凫王朝。

　　1986年7月至9月，震撼世界的奇迹终于出现了。在广汉市南兴镇三星堆周围，先后发掘出两座大型祭祀坑(1号坑约在公元前14世纪，2号坑约在公元前11世纪)，被认为是鱼凫时期的祭祀坑。共出土上千件青铜器精品和大量的金器、玉石礼器、兵器、亚洲象牙等珍贵文物。金杖、青铜立人像、青铜人面像、青铜神树、青铜纵目面具、黄金面罩等等，国之瑰宝，稀世珍品，琳琅满目，美轮美奂。两个祭祀坑的珍贵文物，不仅在巴蜀文化和四川地方史研究方面占有极为重要的地位，而且填补了中国先秦史、中国考古学、中国青铜文化、以及中国冶金史、工艺史、美术史上过去曾出现过的重大空白，对探索中国文明的起源，研究古蜀国的政治、经济、军事、思想和宗教观念、礼仪制度都具有十分重要的价值。

　　历史总是在经过沉淀之后才更具有魅力、更具有穿越时空的悠久美。几千年后，古蜀王国把它辉煌的物质文化展现在现代文明的面前。在世界青铜器时代考古史中，只有埃及、希腊才有出土的真人大小的青铜人雕像、真人头部大小的青铜人头雕像、真人面部大小的黄金面罩，如今中国也发现了这些文物，与埃及、希腊并美于世。那些曾为古希腊青铜器文明钦佩不已的西方学者，面对三星堆遗址的大型青铜雕像的传真照片，更是瞠目结舌，不住颔首称道。英国学者戴维·基斯于1987年8月在英国《独立报》上发表题为《中国青铜雕像无与伦比》的评论文章，称赞"广汉的发现可能是一次出土金属文化最多的发现，它们的发现可能会使人们对东方艺术重新评价。"伦敦不列颠博物馆的首席中国考古学专家杰西卡·罗森则认为："这些发现看来比有名的中国兵马俑更是非同凡响。"四川大学博物馆馆长童恩正教授亦郑重指出："这简直是世界奇迹。"

　　三星堆遗址，是名副其实的世界奇迹。它安居于富饶的川西平原，广汉市西约8公里处南兴镇三星村是它美丽的家园。北面有清澈的鸭子河由西北向东盘桓流过，而宽达数十米的马牧河则由

西南向东涓涓流淌，形成中国西南的"两河流域文明"(两河流域即美索不达米亚，在叙利亚东部和伊拉克境内，曾建有巴比伦、亚述等古国)。在马牧河的南岸原有三处高出地面的黄土堆，像三颗金星一样分布在三星村的东南面，成为三星堆遗址的重要标志。在马牧河的北岸就是与三星堆并称的月亮湾(真武村)。它们隔河相望，为一个整体，有"三星伴月"的美誉。

三星堆遗址，是由6个大的遗址区域组成的大型遗址群，总面积达12平方公里。其中的古城遗址总面积达2.6平方公里，东、西、南部的巨大城墙长达2810米。发掘面积达500平方米。遗址内共出土各类古文物十万余件，内涵丰富，制作精美，造型奇特，引人深思。

三星堆一、二号坑出土青铜器近千件，其中有国宝级6件。拥有青铜人物雕像、人头像、人面像、兽面像、动植物雕像以及黄金面罩、青铜神树、金杖等，各种造型，五光十色，光怪陆离，构筑成一个既雄浑、凝重、而又庄严肃穆的巨大青铜空间，处处充溢着神秘诡谲的远古王国气氛，显示了三千多年前古蜀艺术家们的高超铸造技术和完美的雕塑艺术水平。这些青铜雕像及金杖，艺术风格来源于西亚、近东文明，是中外文化交流的结晶。西亚、近东是青铜雕像和权杖的渊薮，在全球最早进入青铜时代，并有向南亚连续传播分布的历史。联系到三星堆出土的海贝、象牙等，故而雕像、金杖的文化艺术风格不同程度地借鉴了西亚、近东的青铜艺术。同时也借鉴了中原青铜器的某些形式，但从整体来看，仍然具有自成一体的发展特点和结构框架，是中华文化的又一起源地，是古代长江上游的一大文明中心。

三星堆出土的石器有斧、锛、铲、凿、刀、纺轮等。陶器以灰陶为主，红陶次之，多为轮制，火候不甚高，胎骨较松，器形主要有高柄豆、杯、罐、盆、盘等。这里的新石器文化遗址，与龙山文化、齐家文化、二里头文化(夏文化)都有一定的关系，大约在4000年前，其时代大致相当于夏商时期。它与古埃及金字塔、古希腊、古罗马、两河流域、古印度文化相媲美，几乎是人类文明同一季节盛开的鲜花。它把古蜀的历史推前了2000年，使长江流域上游文明与黄河流域文明并驾齐驱，共同成为中华民族的发祥地，因而具有划时代的伟大意义。考古学家的辛勤劳动证明，三星堆这座在地下藏匿了几十个世纪的大都邑，是商代古蜀王国的政治、经济、文化中心，是一个拥有灿烂青铜文化的文明古国。

三星堆祭祀坑，犹如一个威严的地下王国，巨大的青铜人像统治着这个富庶繁荣的冥间世界。总之，青铜雕像群所展示的是一个以蜀王为核心的、有着众多族类君长拥戴的统治集团结构。

2000年底至2001年初，我国考古工作者对三星堆遗址进行了跨世纪的考古发掘，以期揭开在族属来源、文化渊源、文明起源、远古外星人杰作与国家形成等方面的不解之谜。待到谜底揭开，山花烂漫时，古老的东方文化艺术必将更放异彩。全国一流的三星堆博物馆，则是展现三星堆文物精品的恢弘豪华阵容之伟大艺术舞台，那自由升腾的螺旋曲线形的博物馆建筑造型，犹如扶摇直上九重天的青铜神树，把中外游人带进了神秘梦幻般的远古艺术天堂。

Preface

Li Bai (701-762), a great poet of the Tang Dynasty, wrote in a verse, "Since Can Cong and Yu Fu put the Shu Kingdom in order, 4,800 years have passed. Few have tried to the border, where a bird track over a high mountain to the west cuts through mountain eyebrows by the crest" Although the verse is exaggerated, people can perceive the long history of the Shu people, whose origin is harder to be probed than the road to climb to the sky. In the long years, the Shu people created a brilliant history, which was discovered by chance. In 1929, three farmers from a family by the surname of Yan in Yueliangwan (now Zhenwu Village) of Nanxing Town, Guanghan City, Sichuan Province, found a heap of colorful jade stones when digging a pit and installing a waterwheel. A total of more than 400 historical relics, including *bis* (round flat pieces of jade with a hole in the center), *zhangs* (jade tablets), *congs* (long hollow pieces of jade with rectangular sides), jade beads, and raw jade stones. The archaeological finds shed light on the history and culture of the ancient Shu Kingdom.

Between the winter of 1933 and the spring of 1934, an archaeological team led by an American professor and Lin Mingjun, a Chinese professor, from the museum of West China University (present-day Sichuan University) carried out excavations in Yueliangwan. The team members brought to light a great wealth of objects and reference materials. In the following several dozen years, archaeologists continued excavations and made important achievements. The site of the city wall on the eastern, western, and southern sides was affirmed. The site of the Shu Kingdom city, one of the five major cities in ancient China, has an area of 2.6 square kilometers, more or less the same as that of the city of the Shang Dynasty (about 1600-1066 B. C.) in Zhengzhou, Henan Province. The excavation of the ruins of a large palace and the tens of thousands of unearthed historical relics attracted people's attention. Among the archaeological finds is the handle of a pottery ladle with a design of a bird's head, which was made 4,000 to 2,500 years ago. The design bears the head of yufu (cornmorant), representing in a totemic form the Yufu tribe and the reign of Yu Fu of the ancient Shu Kingdom.

From July to September 1986, a world-shaking archaeological marvel appeared. Two large sacrificial pits belonging to the ancient Shu Kingdom were discovered. Pit One was dug during the 14th century B. C. and Pit Two, during the 11th century B. C. Some 1,000 exquisite bronze articles as well as a large quantity of gold and jade sacrificial objects, weapons, tusks of *Elephas maximas*, and other historical treasures were brought to light. These include a wooden walking stick wrapped in gold, a bronze standing human figure, a bronze human face, a bronze divine tree, a bronze vertical mask, and a gilded face guard. The historical relics from the two pits hold important position in the study of the history of the Bashu culture and

the local history of Sichuan Province and filled in the gaps in Chinese archaeology and Chinese bronze culture as well as in the annals of Chinese metallurgy, and fine art. They are of great significance to probing the origin of Chinese civilization and studying the politics, economy, military affairs, ideology, religious concept, and etiquette of the Shu Kingdom in ancient China.

After years of sedimentary accretion, history always has greater charm and a lasting beauty that can transcend space and time. Previously, bronze statues of the size of a human figure, bronze heads as big as a human head, and gilded masks of the size of a human face were discovered only in Egypt and Greece. The historical relics unearthed at Sanxingdui are as treasured as those found in Egypt and Greece. Western scholars had their eyes wide open with surprise at the telephotos of the bronze objects from Sanxingdui. In August 1987, a British scholar published an article, acclaiming the archaeological finds at Sanxingdui a discovery of the metal culture probably with the largest quantity of historical relics that might make people to reevaluate the Oriental art. The chief expert in Chinese archaeology at the British Museum in London held that the historical relics unearthed at Sanxingdui are more remarkable than the noted clay figures of warriors and horses from the tomb of the First Emperor of China's Qin Dynasty in Shaanxi Province. Professor Tong Enzheng, director of the Museum of Sichuan University, pointed out, "The discovery is a miracle of the world."

The ruins in Sanxing Village, eight kilometers west of Guanghan City on the fertile Western Sichuan Plain, is indeed a world's miracle. The crystal-clear Yazi River meanders from northwest to east and the several-dozen-meter-wide Mamu River winds its way from southwest to east, forming a "Mesopotamia" in southwest China (Mesopotamia is in eastern Syria and Iraqi, where Babylon, Assyria, and other ancient countries were established). The three loess mounds on the southern bank of the Mamu River that looked like three golden stars in the southeast of Sanxing Village became an important symbol of the ruins at Sanxingdui. On the northern bank of the river is Yueliangwan (Zhenwu Village). The two villages facing each other on the opposite banks by the river are called Sanxingbanyue, meaning three stars accompanying the moon, one of the eight major scenic spots in the area.

The ruins at Sanxingdui consist of six groups of ruins with a total area of 12 square kilometers, including the site of an ancient city that stretches for 2.6 square kilometers. The city wall on the east, west, and south extends 2,810 meters. Some 500 square meters of the ancient city have been excavated, and more than 100,000 historical relics were unearthed. These historical relics are rich in content, novel in design, and of fine workmanship. There are such stone objects as axes, adzes, shovels, chisels,

and spinning wheels. Of the unearthed pottery articles, gray pottery occupies first place and red pottery comes second. Most of the pottery objects are high-stemmed *dous* (bowls), cups, jars, basins, and plates. They were fired in an annular kiln with a loose base, indicating an insufficient duration of heating.

The cultural ruins at Sanxingdui that belong to the Neolithic culture some 4,000 years ago roughly during the Xia (c. 21st-c. 16th century B. C.) and Shang (c. 16th century-1066 B. C.) dynasties are related, to a certain extent, to the Longshan, Qijia, and Erlitou cultures (the culture of the Xia Dynasty). The ruins at Sanxingdui are as old as the Pyramids of ancient Egypt and the civilization of ancient Greece, ancient Rome, Mesopotamia, and ancient India. The discovery of the ruins pushed the history of the ancient Shu Kingdom 2,000 years earlier, showed that the Changjiang River valley is a birthplace of Chinese civilization like the Huanghe River valley, and is of epoch-making significance. Archaeological study testified to the fact that the site of the ancient city was a political, economic, and culture center of the Shu Kingdom with a brilliant bronze culture during the Shang Dynasty.

Of the nearly 1,000 bronze objects that were brought to light from the two pits at Sandxingdui, six are national treasures. There are a bronze mask in the design of a human figure, a bronze human head, a bronze human face, a bronze object with an animal face, bronze objects in the shape of an animal or a plant plus a gilded mask, a bronze divine tree, a gold-wrapped walking stick, showing the superb casting and perfect sculpture technologies of the artists of the ancient Shu Kingdom more than 3,000 years ago. The bronze objects and the gold-wrapped walking sticks were made by drawing on the artistic style of West Asia, the Near East, and central China, a result of the cultural interflow between China and other countries. West Asia and the Near East, birthplaces of bronze figures and gold-wrapped walking sticks, first entered the bronze era in the world and then spread the bronze art to South Asia. When viewing the unearthed bronze objects as a whole, one can find that these bronze objects have a style of their own, testifying that the ruins at Sanxingdui were another birthplace of Chinese culture and a center of civilization on the upper reaches of the Changjiang River.

The bronze objects unearthed from the two sacrificial pits show the structure of the ruling class with the king of the Shu Kingdom as the core, supported by the heads of various clans.

At the end of 2,000 and the beginning of 2001, Chinese archaeologists made another excavation of the ruins at Sanxingdui in a hope to unveil the origin of the clans, their culture and civilization and the formation of the kingdom. A museum has been constructed over the ruins. The museum in a spiral, curved form is a palace of ancient art.

神秘的三星堆博物馆

THE MYSTERIOUS SANXINGDUI MUSEUM, A PROFOUND ART PALACE.

深邃的艺术殿堂

三星堆博物馆。位于三星堆遗址东北角,南距成都30公里,是我国一座新兴的大型现代化历史博物馆。

The Sanxingdui Museum. Located at the northeastern corner of the ruins in Sanxingdui and 30 kilometers north of Chengdu, It is a historical relic under key state protection and a large, new, and modern museum of history.

三星堆遗址重点保护区示意图
Map Showing the Key Spots of the Ruins under Protection at Sanxingdui

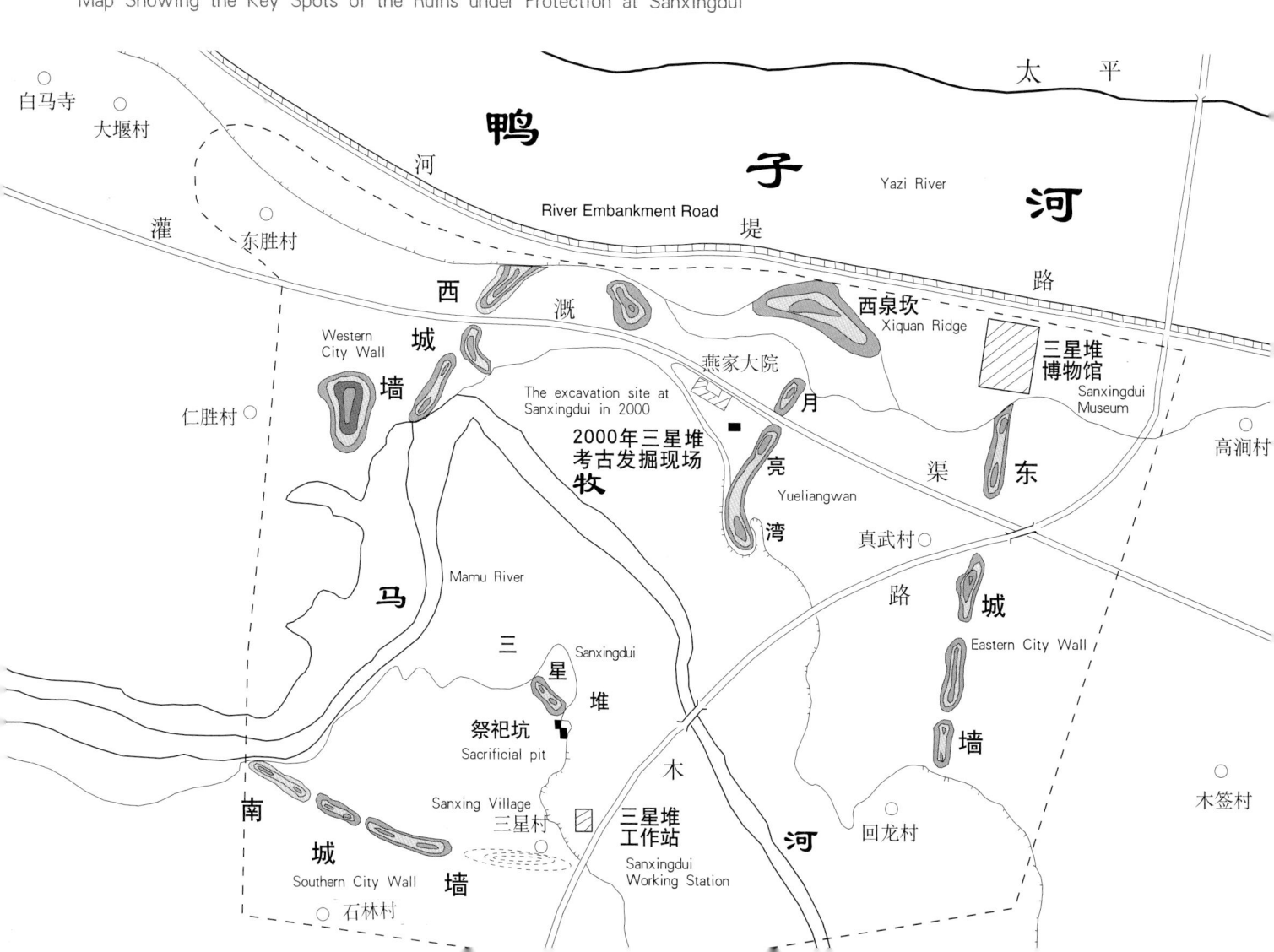

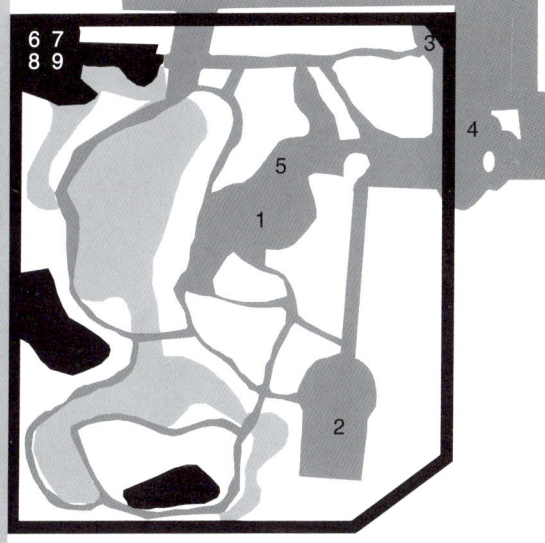

三星堆博物馆参观路线示意图
Map Showing Visitors' Itinerary at Sanxingdui Museum.

1. 三星堆博物馆 Sanxingdui Museum
2. 祭祀台表演场 The Altar for Recreation of the Sacrificial Ceremony
3. 卫生间 Washroom
4. 售票处 Admission Ticket Office
5. 贵宾接待处 Lounge for Honored Guests
6. 派出所 Police Substation
7. 博物馆办公室 Museum Office
8. 餐厅 Dining Hall
9. 纪念品销售处 Keepsake Sales Counter

　　三星堆古蜀国充满了神秘色彩，是有待人们去拓荒、去探求的上古社会的一个缩影。三星堆文物充分体现了那个久远时代的神秘性。那些至今也无人破译的巴蜀图文、图语，这些符号是文字？族徽？图画？还是某种宗教符号？无数个莫测高深的千古之谜，等待人们去索解、去破译。

　　The ancient Shu was a kingdom at Sanxingdui and an epitome of the remote society. Among the unearthed historical relics are a number of symbols, which have not been deciphered yet. Are they pictographs, clan emblems, pictures, or religious symbols? All this remains a mystery.

继一号祭祀坑的发掘,二号祭祀坑在1986年8月也现身于世人眼前。祭祀坑出土数十根象牙,精美的青铜像、金面人头像、玉石器等。其中青铜立人像的出土犹引人注目,是中国考古史上所发掘出的最大型人像。雕刻精细、造型写实,极具夸张成分。

In August 1986, the second sacrificial pit was excavated following the excavation of the first sacrificial pit. Unearthed were several dozen elephant tusks, exquisite bronze human figures, human heads with a gilded face, and stone and jade objects. The excavation of the bronze human figure in a standing position became the center of special attention. Exquisitely carved, in a realistic shape, and of extremely exaggerated, it is the largest of its kind ever found in the annals of Chinese archaeology.

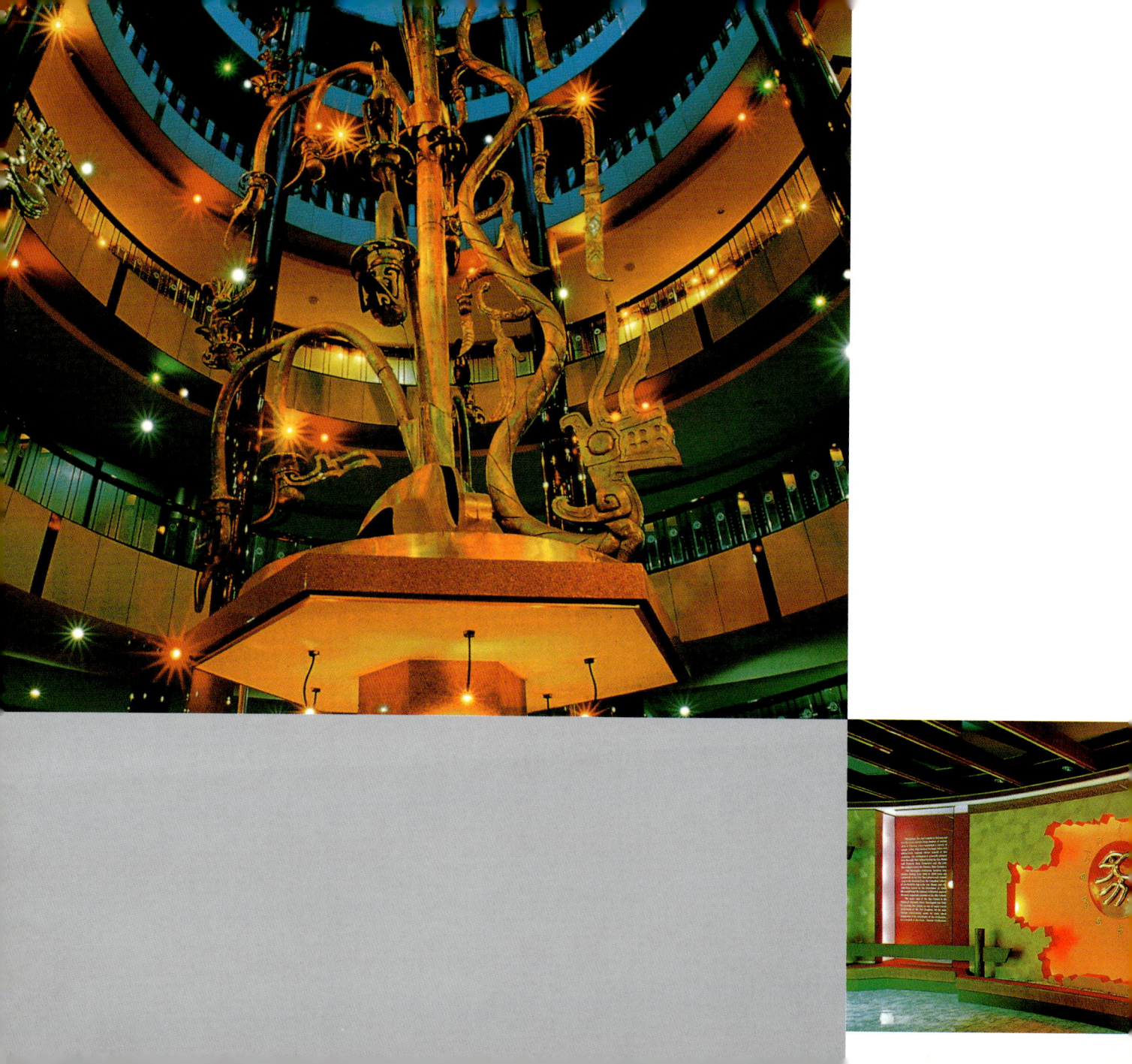

博物馆全景式立体陈列的手法。通过多层次、多视角、全方位的展示手段，给人们一种新的感觉及美的享受。

A panoramic display of exhibits at the museum has brought about a new visual effect.

博物馆外观环境优美、地势开阔、空气清新，现代园林环境与周围自然形态巧妙的融为一体，突出了博物馆多元化发展趋向与综合性的服务功能。

The museum features a beautiful environment with an open space, fresh air, an integration of the modern gardening environment and the natural scenery, and a stress on a diversified development and comprehensive service function.

神秘　诡谲

MYSTERIOUS, ECCENTRIC, ASTONISHING, AND EXCELLENT.

惊异　叹绝

青铜立人像，是三星堆青铜器的代表作，像高1.7米，底座0.9米，共达2.6米，是三星堆最大一尊铜像，也是中国迄今发现的最大的一座青铜人像。头带花冠，阔眉，杏叶眼，双手抬于肩高作握物状，身着长襟"燕尾"服。服装上饰以凤鸟、兽面和云气纹，左肩右斜饰一"法带"，立于由怪兽承起的"法坛"上，当为巫师形象。

A bronze figure in a standing posture, 2.6 meters high (1.7 meters for the figure and 0.9 meters for the altar). It is the largest bronze figure found in Sanxingdui. Standing on an altar with a strange animal support, the figure has broad eyebrows and almond-shaped eyes and wears a corolla and a swallow-tailed coat with a long front. A "magic" band hangs slantingly to the right from the left shoulder. The coat is embroidered with phoenix, animal's head, and cloud patterns. It is believed to be a sorcerer.

22 三星堆 SANXINGDUI

1. 失冠A型人头像。头顶为子母口型，原来应有冠饰套接其上。残高29公分。
   A human head with the cap missing. There is a joint on the top of the head. Originally, there should be a cap joining the head. The remaining part is 29cm high.
2. C型人头像。头顶呈圆形，人头像头发由后往前梳，饰蝴蝶形花结。整体形象壮严肃穆。高37公分。
   A human head with a round top is 37cm high. The hair was combed forward from behind and decorated with a bowknot. It has a solemn facial expression.
3. 青铜人面像。三星堆遗址的两座祭祀坑中出土了二十余件青铜人面像，大小各异，像宽从10余公分至60公分不等，但面容结构相似。其作用是在宗教活动中用于祭祀祈祝。
   Bronze figures with a human face. More than 20 bronze figures with a human face were brought to light from the two sacrificial pits. Varied in size and width they are from 10cm to 60cm across but have a similar structure. They were used at sacrificial ceremonies or prayers in religious activities.

纵目兽面像。出土于二号祭祀坑,商代前期遗物。面部为长方形,角尺状大兽耳,向两侧开展。圆菱柱状眼球,向前伸出,鹰勾鼻,阔口,其综合表现出许多动物的特征,为多种动物的结合体。是蜀人崇拜的天神和祖宗神。高65公分,宽138公分。

A bronze object in the shape of an animal head with protruding eyes, made during the early stage of the Shang Dynasty and unearthed from the second sacrificial pit. It is 65cm high and 138cm across. It has a rectangular face, two large horn-like ears erecting to the sides, two cylindrical eyeballs, a hawk nose, and a wide mouth, showing the characteristics of various animals. It was the heavenly god and ancestral god worshipped by the people of the Shu Kingdom.

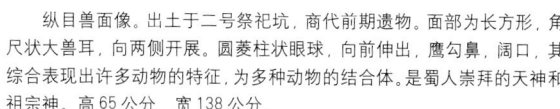

1. D型人头像。头顶上带有索状圆箍，整体轮廓明显，线条分明。高13.5公分。
   A human head with a rope-like round hoop on top is 13.5cm high and has a distinct contour and clear lines.
2. A型失冠人头像。残高17.5公分。
   A dignified human head with the cap missing. The remaining height is 17.5cm.
3. B型人头像。头似戴双角形头盔，头盔下有头套将颈部套住，表情威严，头顶有铸造时铜液滞流而形成的孔洞。高46.7公分。
   A human head, 46.7cm high. It seems that the head is in a helmet with two horns. Underneath is a headgear linking the neck. On the top of the head, there is a hole left by the viscous flow of the melted bronze.

1. 跪坐人像。三星堆一号、二号坑出土了许多跪坐小人像，高约十几公分不等，有的张口露齿神态严肃，有的正襟危坐表情肃穆，这些人像均为祭祀中巫祝的代表。
   Many small bronze human figures in a kneeling posture were found in the two pits. They are more or less about 10cm high. Some of them have their mouths open and teeth exposed and bear a serious manner, others are sitting rigidly upright. They were believed to be representatives of the one who prayed to gods for blessing the people at sacrificial ceremonies.

2. 带冠小人像
   A small human head with cap.

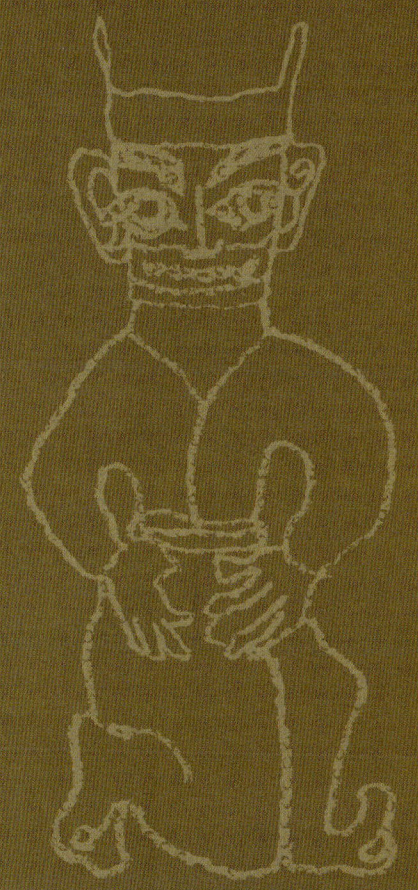

1. C型人头像。出土时颈部被火烧熔化向上反卷。残高37.5公分。
   A human head with a remaining height of 37.5cm. The neck was burned to turn upward at the time of excavation.
2. A型人头像。威严的神色中又可见微然笑意。高41.2公分。
   A human head, dignified yet smiling, 41.2cm high.
3. C型人头像。头呈平顶状,似带平顶帽。残高37.5公分。
   A human head with a flat top, seemingly with a flat-topped cap. The remaining height is 37.5cm.
4. B型人头像。头带回字纹平顶冠,面部戴有面罩。头发敛于冠内。高34.7公分。
   A human head with a fret design, flat-topped cap and a mask, 34.7cm high. The hair is held in the cap.

三星堆 SANXINGDUI

4

三星堆 SANXINGDUI

2

1. 戴冠纵目兽面像。额头正中有一以补铸法安装的额饰。呈夔龙状，外卷角，身、尾向上内卷。装饰华美。通高83公分。
   A bronze mask in the shape of an animal head and with protruding eyes and a body like the one-legged monster in fable, 83cm in overall height. The horns roll up outward and the body and tail, inward. In the middle of the forehead, there is an ornament made by topping-up casting.

2. 夔龙兽面。有兽面和夔龙两部分组成。表情滑稽，下颌转角处各有一个作固定使用的小圆孔。为祭祀活动中所带的面具。宽22.6公分。
   A bronze mask, 22.6 across, is composed of two parts — the one-legged monster in fable and an animal head. There is a round hole in each of the corners of the lower jaw to fix the mask in position. It was a mask worn at sacrifice-offering ceremonies.

1. 人面像
   A human face.
2. 夔龙兽面
   A mask in the shape of an animal head with a design of the one-legged monster in fable.

1

1. 人头像
   A human head.
2. 夔龙兽面
   An animal head-shaped mask with a design of the one-legged monster in fable.
3. 人面像
   Human faces.

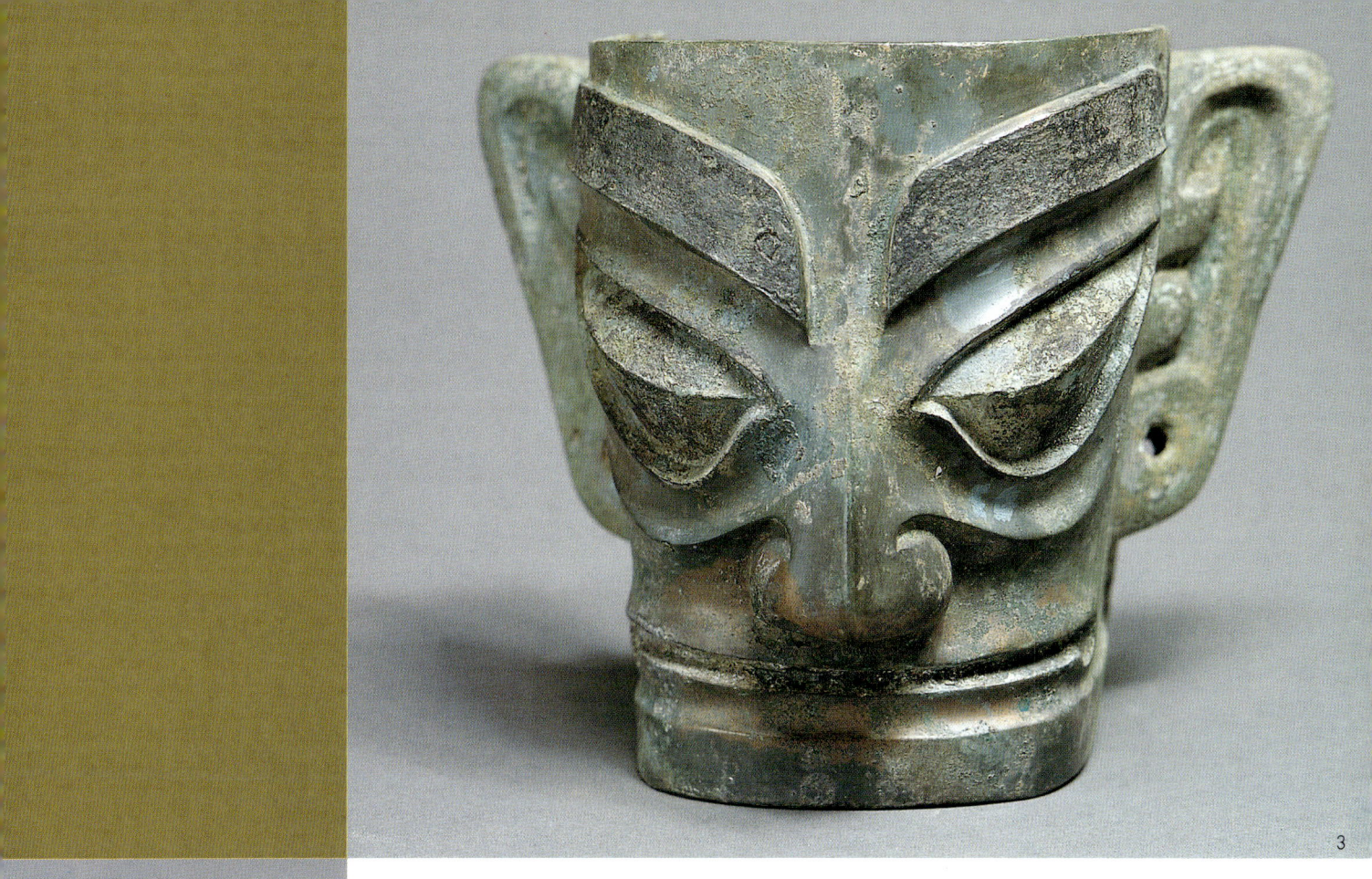

人面像
A human faced mask.

三星堆 SANXINGDUI 39

40 三星堆 SANXINGDUI

1. 人面像
    A human faced-mask.
2. 人面像
    A human faced-mask.
3. A型人头像
    A human head.

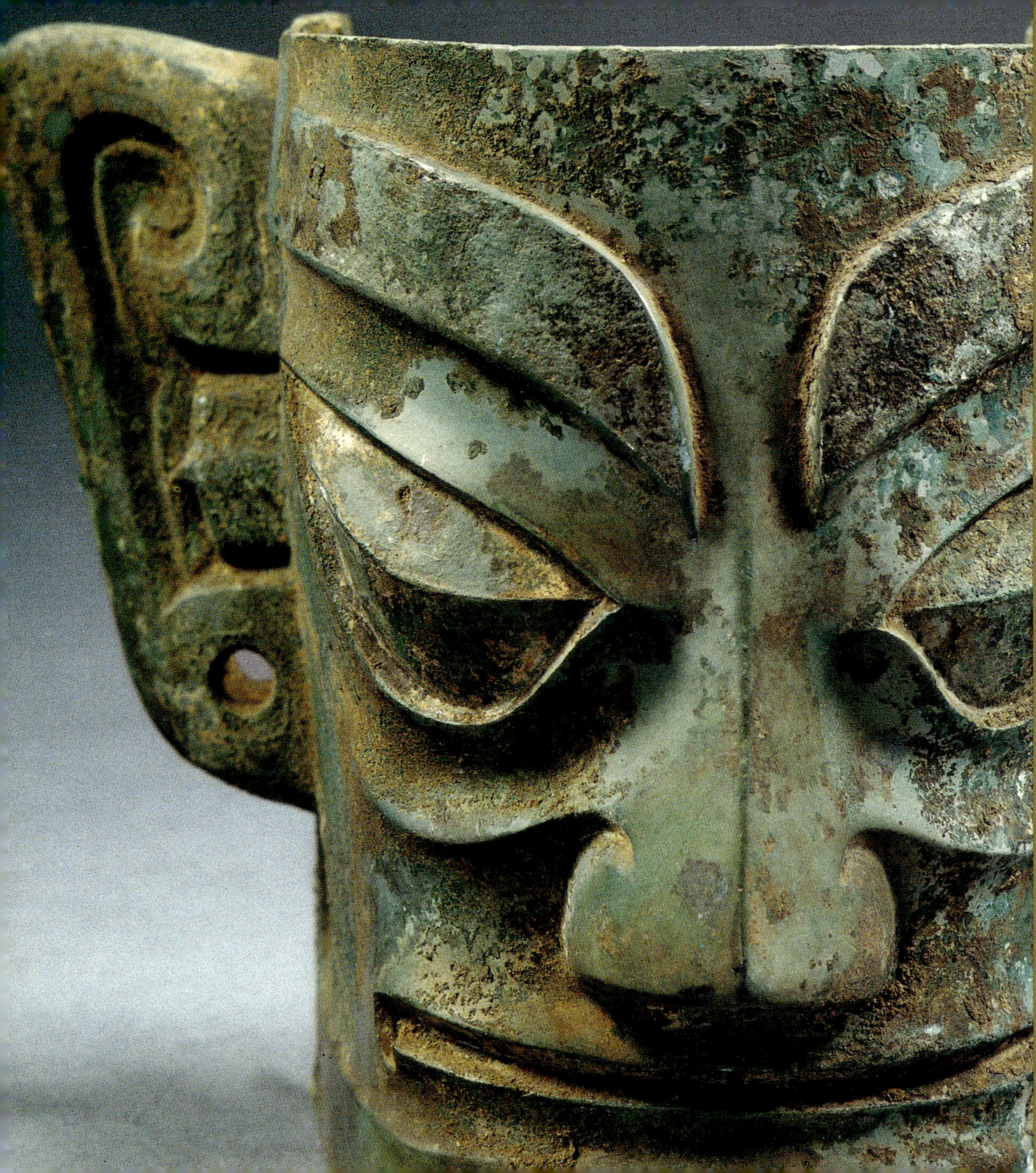

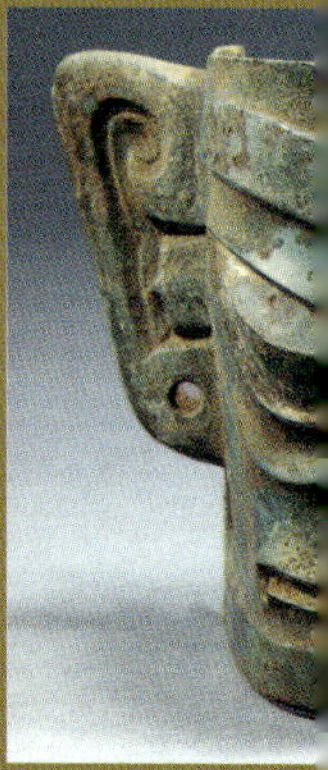

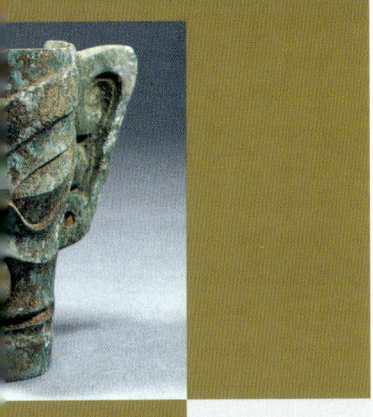

各种人面像
Various masks with a human face.

夔龙兽面
An animal head-shaped mask with a design of the one-legged monster in fable.

三星堆 SANXINGDUI 45

1. 人头像
   A human head.
2. A型人头像背面。头发向后梳理，编成发辫，辫上端扎束。
   A view of the back of the human head. The hair was combed backward into braid and tied up at the upper end.
3. 人面像
   A human faced-mask.
4. 夔龙兽面
   A mask in the shape of an animal head with a design of the one-legged monster in fable.

三星堆 SANXINGDUI

4

烈火熔金

GOLD MELTED IN FIRE; HEAVEN, EARTH, AND THE GODS.

天地神灵

金面罩。出土时因受到其他文物的挤压，而皱成一团。有的甚至于残破断裂，但仍能从形状、大小和制作工艺上看出，它与金面人头像上的金面罩大致相同。因此，也应该有各自的人头像与之相配。

A gold mask. It was creased and damaged when unearthed because of the pressure of other historical relics. It is roughly similar to the unearthed gold mask of the bronze human head with a gilded face in shape, size, and workmanship. Therefore, there should be a bronze human head to form a complete set with it.

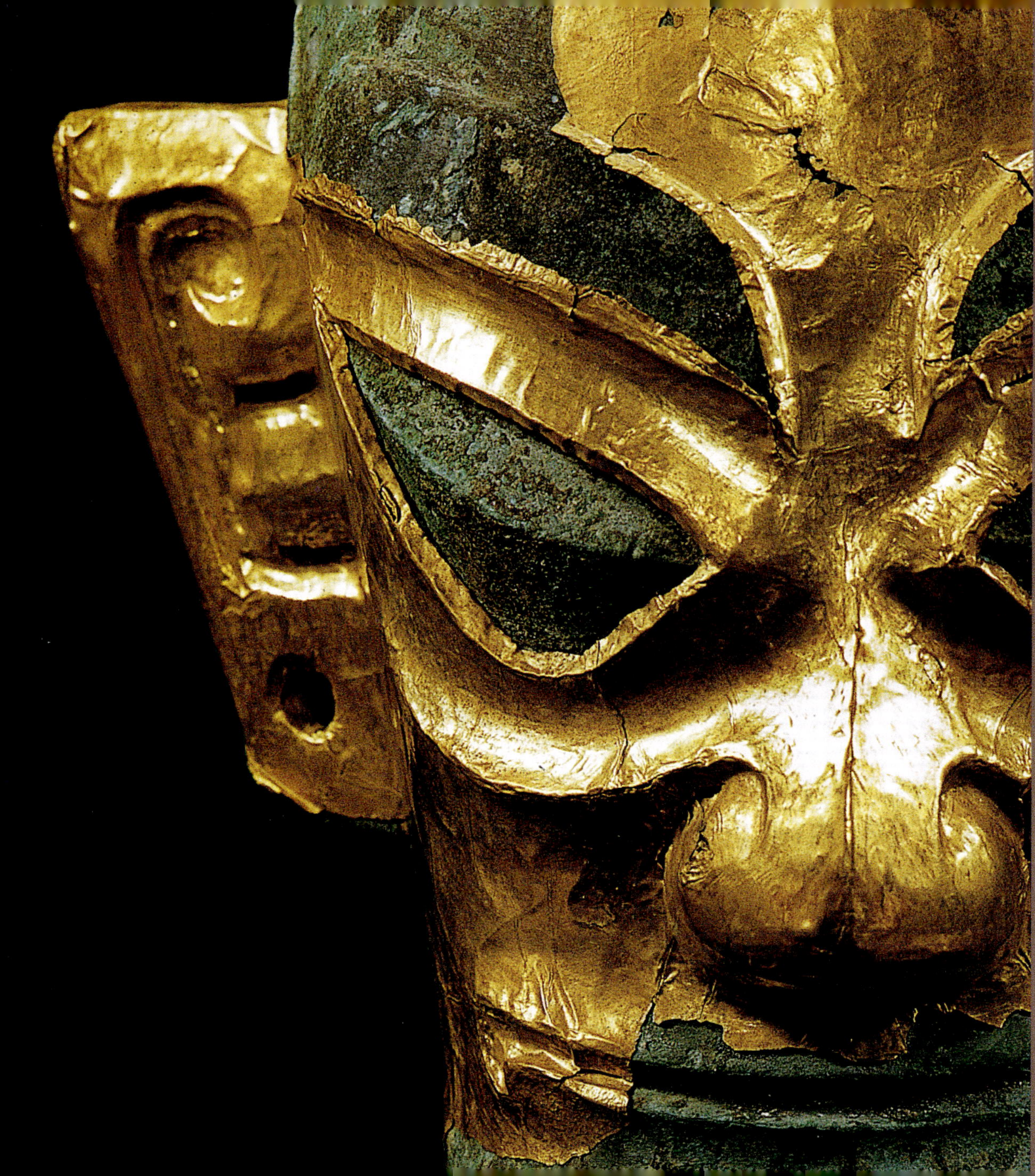

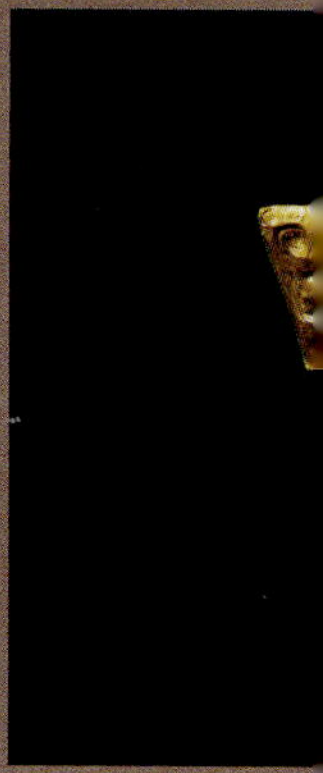

金面铜人头像。由铜头像和金面罩两部分组成。人头像为圆头顶,面部戴着面罩蒙至头顶,面罩上又铸出和金面罩大小相同的轮廓线。倒八字长眉,杏核状丹凤眼,蒜头鼻,鼻梁较短。阔口,闭唇。宽方颐,长条形耳廓,耳垂有一穿孔。青铜人头像与金面罩紧密闭合。造型、大小均与人头像相同。

A bronze human head with a gold mask. The shape and size of the head are similar to that of a real human head. It features a round top, almond-shaped eyes, a garlic bulb-like nose, a short nose bridge, a big mouth with the lips closed, a broad forehead, and long ears. There is a hole in each of the two earlobes. The eyebrows are in the shape of the inverted Chinese character 八. The gold mask is outlined with bronze covers closely on to the bronze head.

52 三星堆 SANXINGDUI

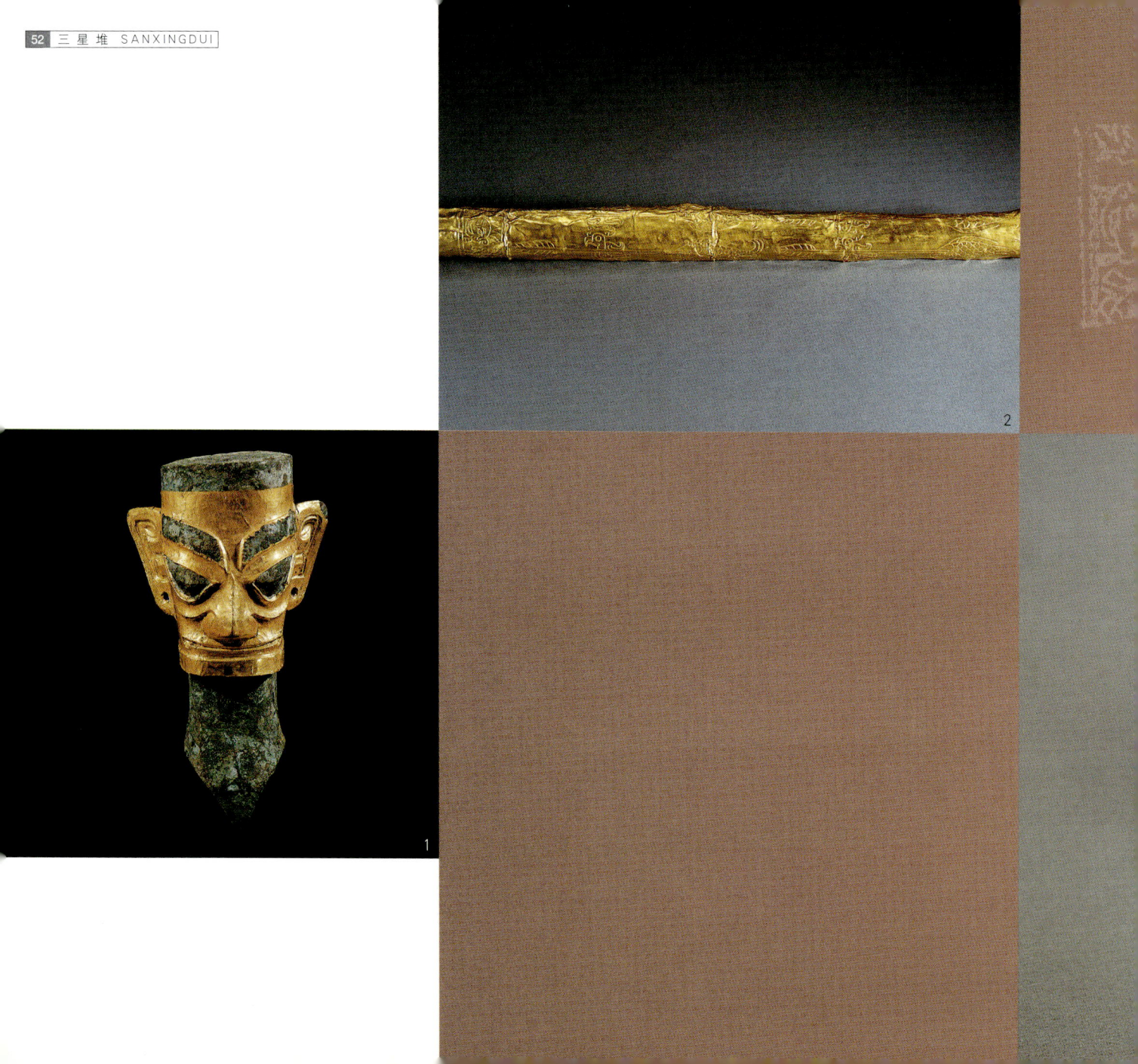

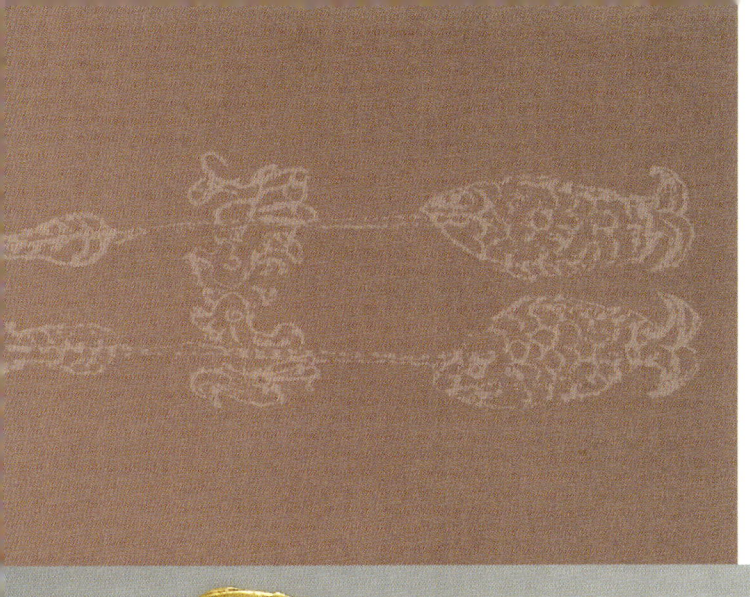

1. 金面人头像
   A bronze human head with a gilded face.
2. 金杖。用纯金皮包卷而成，其有上端有平雕纹饰图案。图案内刻有人物、鱼鸟和剑等，在鱼的头部和鸟的颈部各压有一只箭，似表现鸟驮负着被箭射中的鱼，飞翔而来的场面。金杖应是巫祝之类的人物所使用的法器。长142公分，直径2.3公分。
   A gold-wrapped stick, 142cm long and 2.3cm in diameter. The upper part bears the pattern of a human figure, a fish, a bird, and a sword. There is an arrowhead over both the fish and the neck of the bird seemingly to show that the bird is carrying the fish hit by the arrow. The gold-wrapped stick is believed to be a ritual object of the one who prayed to gods for blessing the people.
3. 金箔虎形器。虎头昂起，口大张，做咆啸状，眼镂空，前足伸，后足蹲，形象十分生动、逼真。长11.7公分。
   A goldleaf object in the shape of a tiger, 11.7cm long. The life-like tiger has a raised head, opened mouth, and hollowed-out eyes. One of the forepaws is outstretching while the hind paws are in a crouching position.

通天神树

THE DIVINE TREE STANDS SKY HIGH TO LINK MEN AND THE GODS

沟通人神

青铜神树,由底座和树身两部分组成。其树高3.48米,是全世界最大的出土青铜器。底座上铸有三个跪坐守卫的人,高大的枝干上有茂盛的枝叶、花卉、果实,还有飞禽、走兽、悬龙、挂铃等。这满身生长奇物的神树,造型庞大,它像征的是一条通天神道。右图为神树中的饰件。

composed a base and the tree itself. The base consists of three kneeling guards and the huge tree features luxuriant foliage laden with flowers, fruit, birds, animals, and bells, symbolizing the divine road to heaven.

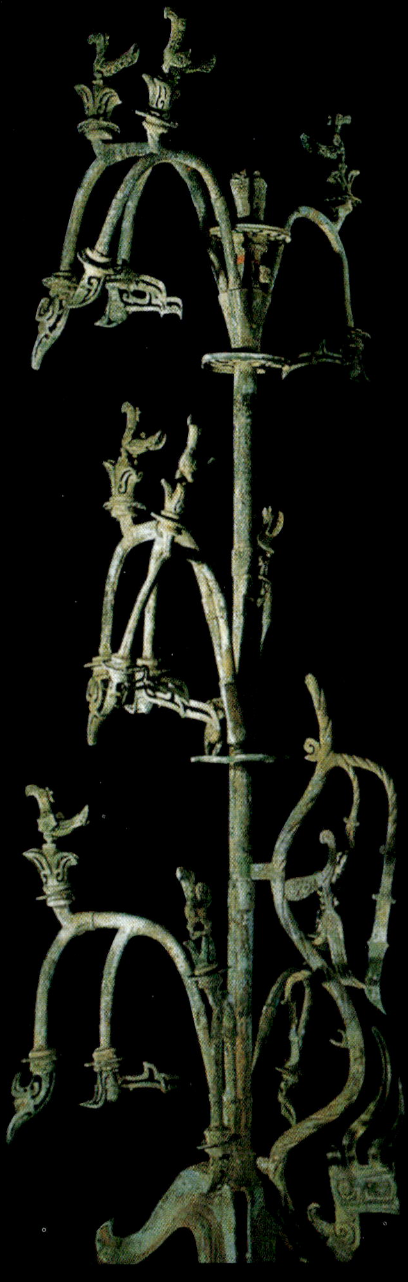
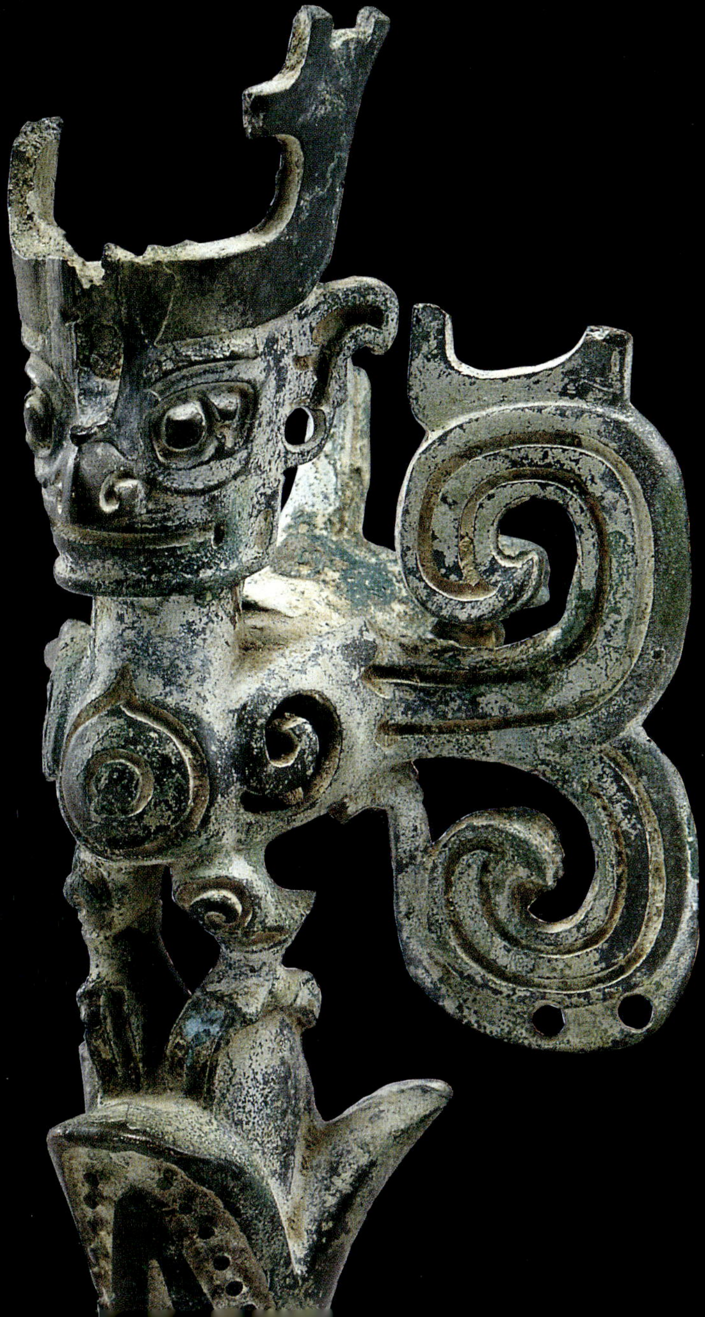

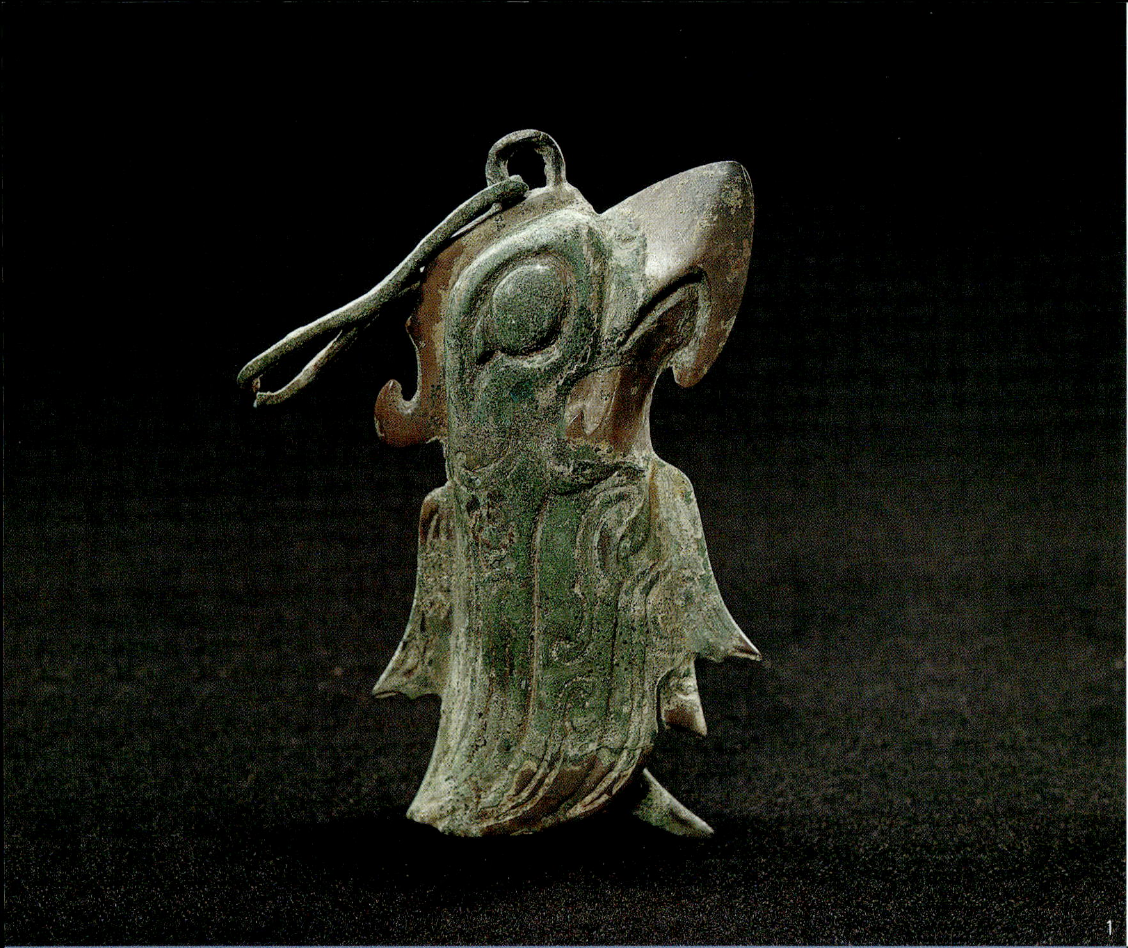

1

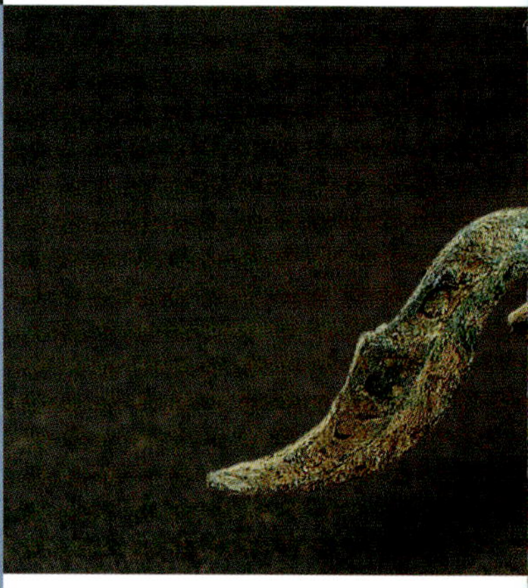

1. 鹰形铃。铃作鹰蹲栖状,两面有羽状纹理。高14公分。
   A bell in the shape of a sitting hawk, with feather-like patterns on the sides. It is 14cm high.
2. 虎形器
   An object in the shape of a tiger.
3. 鹰头饰。该器成鹰头状,断面为椭圆形。此物外形奇特,功用不明,推测可能为建筑饰件。高40.3公分。
   An ornament in the shape of a hawk's head, with an oval-shaped cross section, 40.3cm high. It was inferred to be an architectural ornament.

58 | 三星堆 SANXINGDUI

三星堆 SANXINGDUI

各种凤头凤尾鸟形器
Ornaments in the shape of a bird with a phoenix's head and tail.

虎形器。虎方头昂首，双眼圆睁，张口露齿，竖尾，但尾尖已残，虎身肥而硕大，四足立于圆座之上，造型憨厚，令人玩味。高11公分。

An ornament in the shape of a tiger, 11cm high. The tiger, with a large, fat body and a silly disposition, stands on a round base. It holds its head high, opens its eyes wide, shows its teeth, and raises its tail. The tip of the tail is incomplete.

三星堆 SANXINGDUI 61

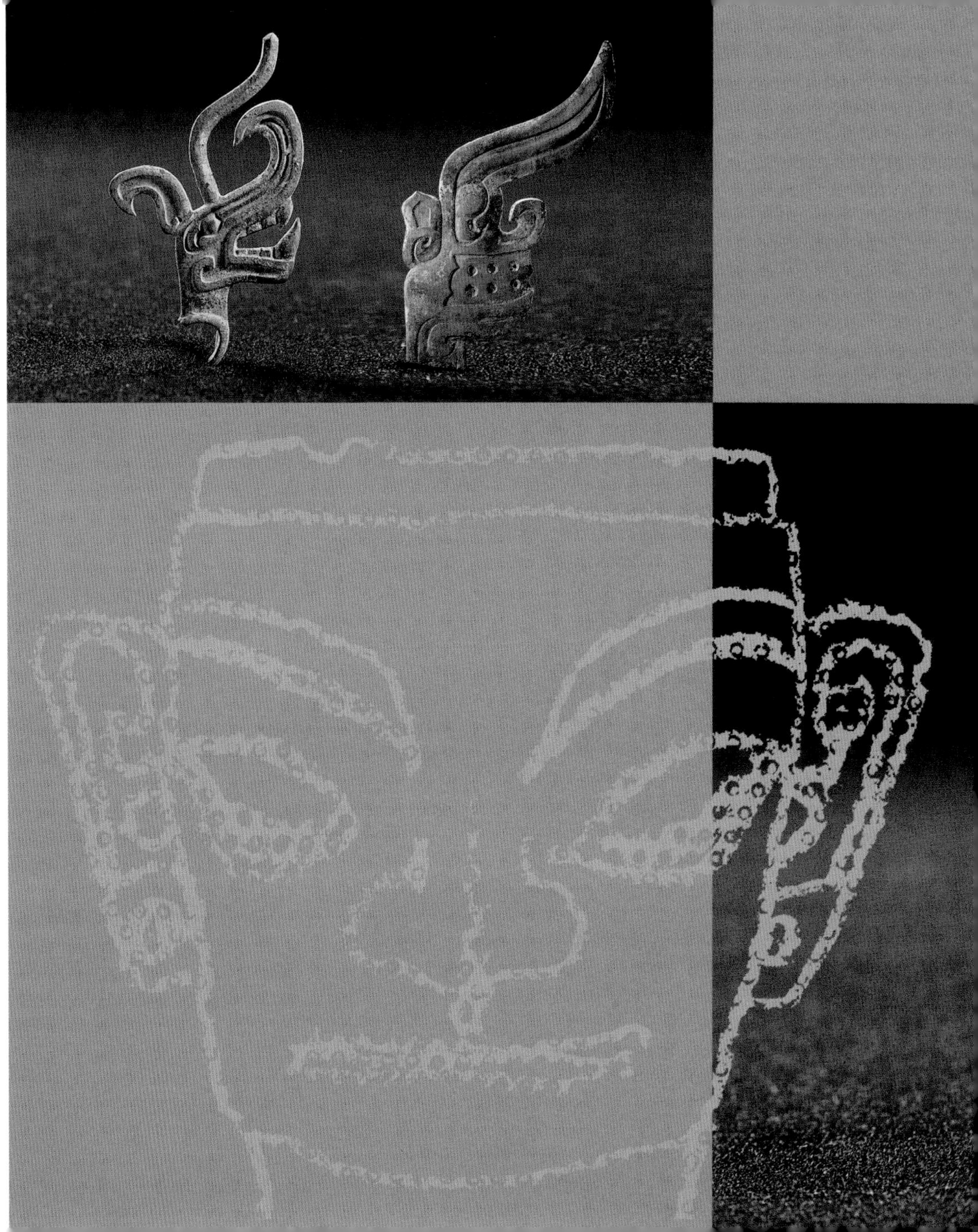

各种鸟形、凤形、夔龙饰。为青铜镂空造型,不以写实为主,而以线条表现鸟、凤的各种造型。多为某种器物的配件。

Hollowed-out bronze ornaments in the shape of birds and phoenix. Most of them were fittings of various objects.

64 三星堆 SANXINGDUI

各种铜鸟、凤器物。三星堆遗址出土了数以百计的鸟、凤类造型的青铜器。他们大多属于一些器物上的附件。这反映了古蜀族的鸟崇拜的实质是对太阳神崇拜。人们崇拜太阳的目的是祈祷丰收。

Hundreds of bronze articles in the form of birds and phoenix were brought to light at Sanxingdui, and most of them were attachments to other objects, showing the worship for the bird by the people of the ancient Shu Kingdom. The bird worship is, in nature, the worship for the god of the sun in the hope of good harvest.

铜鸡。由造型可知此为雄鸡,高冠、引颈、昂首、身体肥硕、尾羽丰满。造型生动,颇具写实风格。

This bronze rooster is true to life with a large comb, a raised head, a fully-fledged tail, and a body.

三星堆 SANXINGDUI

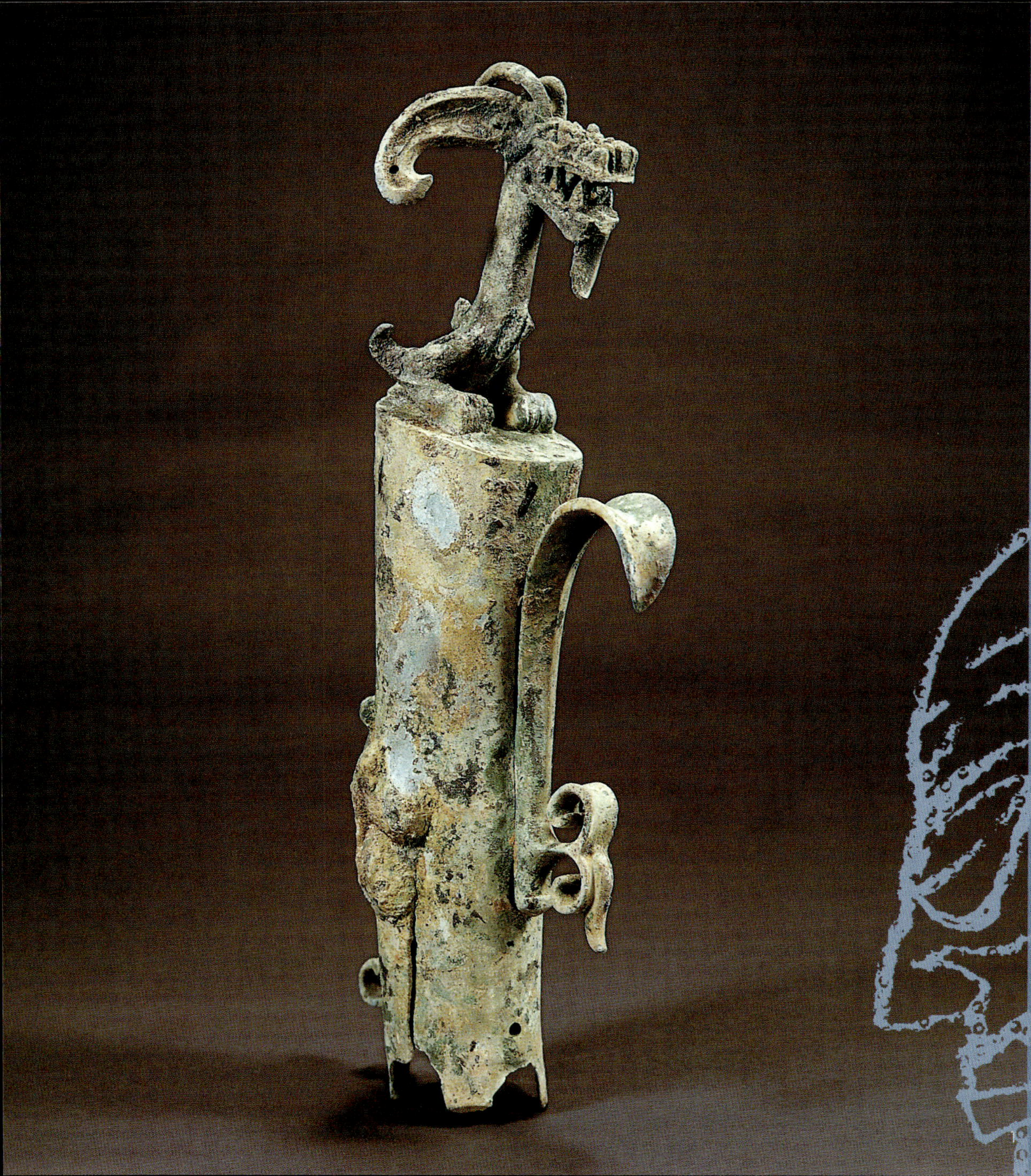

1. 爬龙柱形器。猫科身躯但弯角大耳，突目鼻，阔嘴锐牙，颌下有须。尾部垂于铜柱上。人和动物复合的造型可以叫做怪物或神物。这些神物带领我们进入另外一个世界，那里可能是我们远古祖先的故乡，也可能是人类心灵最深层的终极归宿。高41公分。
   A pillar-shaped object with a dragon design, 41cm high. It has a felid body, curved horns, big ears, a large mouth, sharp teeth, whiskers on the lower jaw, and a tail hanging from the bronze pillar. It is a combination of human being and the animal, known as a monster or a supernatural being. It can introduce us to another world, which might have been the home of our ancestors in remote antiquity or the ultimate destination deep in people's hearts.

2. 擎物跪坐像
   A figure kneeling down on a tree-shaped base.

3. 蛇形饰。长54公分。
   A snake-shaped ornament, 54cm long.

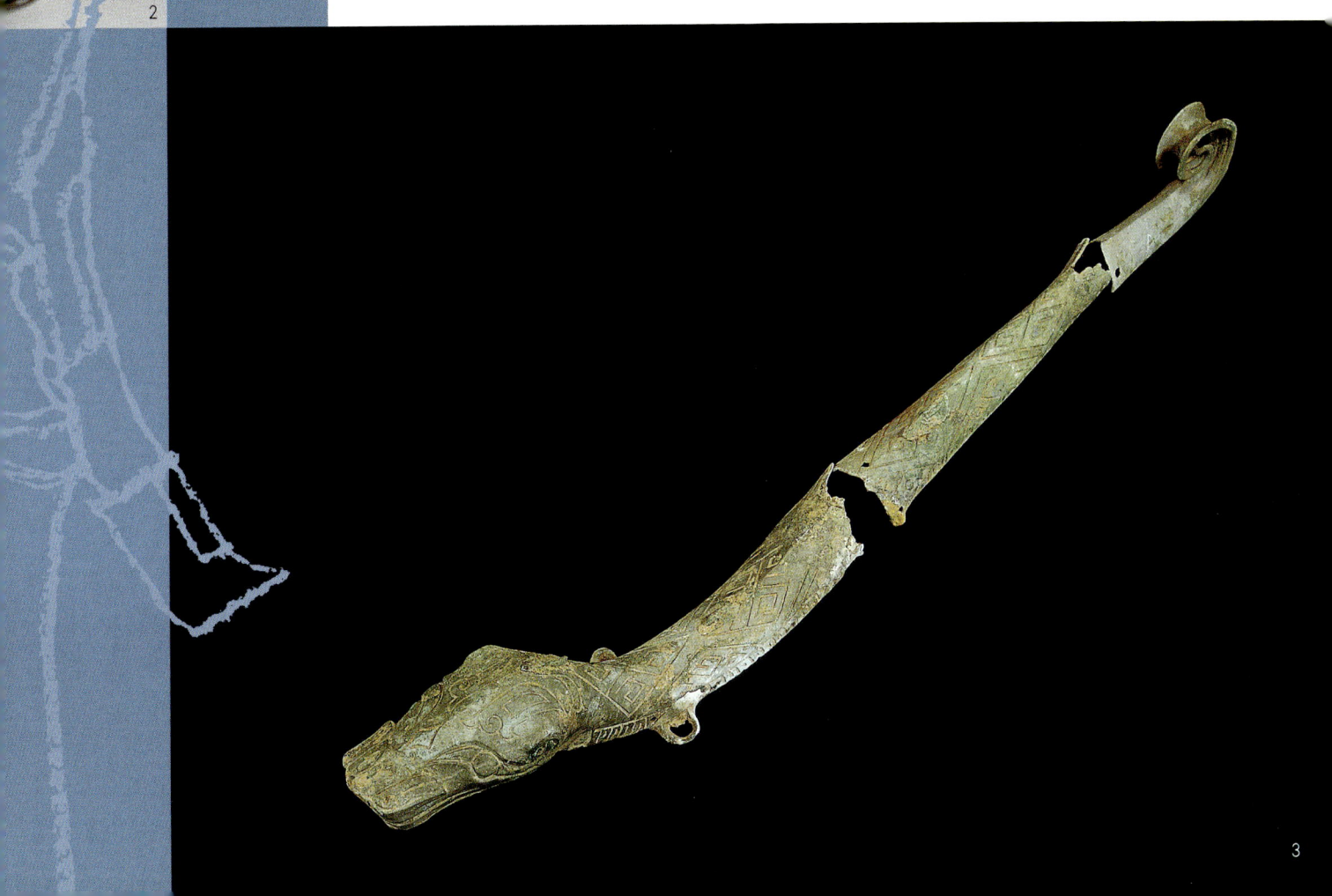

三星堆 SANXINGDUI

1

1. 铜贝。三枚成套。上端有三个环钮并联。长5公分。
   Bronze cowries, 5cm long each. The set of three are connected with loops on the upper part.
2. 铜玲局部纹饰。桶形，两面以兽面纹为装饰，兽面为立眼，内卷角，身、尾卷于后部。宽7公分。
   The design on part of a bronze bell. The sides are decorated with an animal pattern with horns rolled up inward and the body and tail huddled up at the back.

各式各样的眼形器、眼泡、太阳形器。这些青铜器多有各种穿孔，可能是与其他饰物配合使用的附件。

Eye-, eyeball- and sun-shaped bronze objects. Most of them have holes in them. They were probably fittings of other ornaments.

三星堆 SANXINGDUI 73

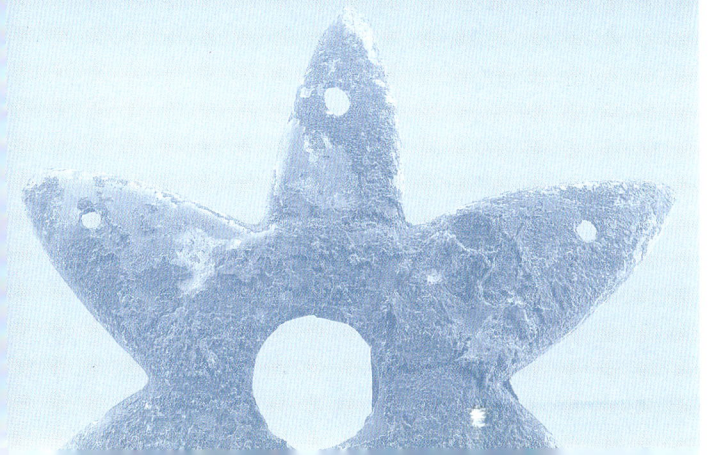

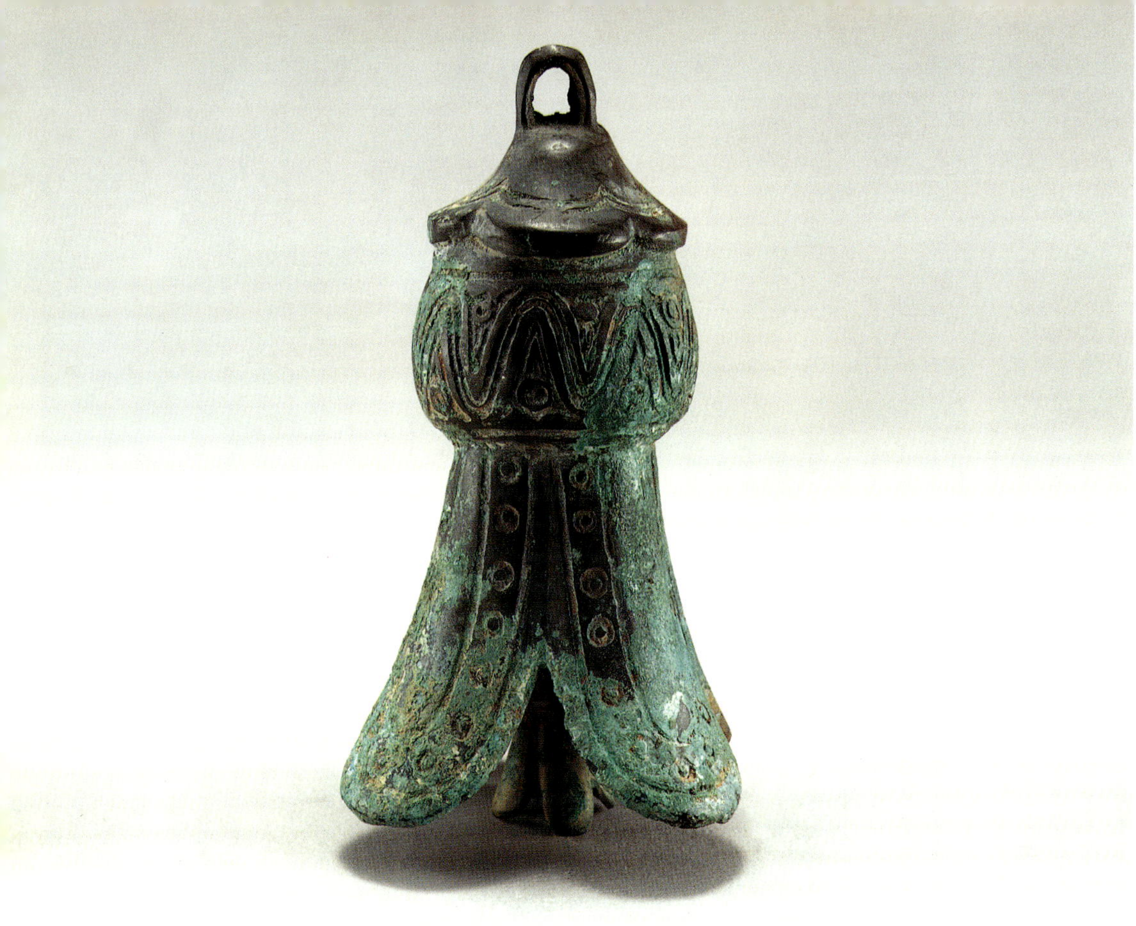
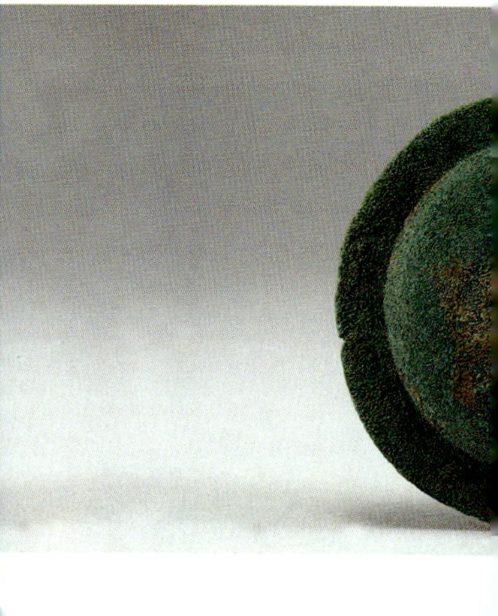

各种花果形、兽面形铜铃。多为其他器物的挂件,种类繁多、造型精美。高约10公分左右。

Bronze bells in the shape of flowers, fruit, or animals. Most of them were exquisite pendants of other ornaments and are about 10cm high.

龙虎尊局部图案
Part of the dragon and tiger design on a *zun*, an ancient wine vessel.

三 星 堆 SANXINGDUI

78　三星堆 SANXINGDUI

1. 六鸟三牛尊。高 56.5 公分。
   A *zun* bearing a design of six birds and three oxen, 56.5cm high.
2. 四鸟四兽罍。高 54 公分。
   A *lei*, an ancient container with a design of four birds and four animals, 54cm high.
3. 六鸟三牛尊。高 40.5 公分。
   A *zun* with a design of six birds and three oxen, 40.5cm high.

镂石攻玉

CARVED STONES AND JADE FOR CEREMONIAL
PURPOSES ALL OVER THE LAND

礼天地四方

玉琮。黄绿色半透明。器身内圆外方，四面各刻有五条平行线。造型简洁大方。高 7.2 公分。

Zong is a yellowish-green translucent square jade object with a round hole in the cener and is 7.2cm high. It is simple in design and graceful in style. There are five parallel lines on each of the four sides.

1

1. 玉瑗。直径 10.5 公分。
   Yuan, a round flat piece of jade with a big hole in the center, 10.5cm in diameter.
2. 玉珠。有翠绿、碧绿、牙黄、深灰等多种色彩，大小不等，大多为鼓形，其中极少数为算珠形，共 40 颗。
   A string of 40 emerald-green, dark-green, ivory-yellow, and dark-gray pearls of every size. Most of them are drum-shaped, a few are in the shape of an abacus bead.
3. 玉璧。直径 13.7 公分。
   Bi, a round flat piece of jade with a hole in its center used for ceremonial purposes in ancient China, 13.7cm in diameter.

1

1,2. 玉璋。黑色不透明。上有多组人形图案，均头戴平顶帽，双手做揖状。玉璋是用来祭祀天地四方中礼南方的器物。

Zhang, a jade tablet, is non-transparent black in color. It was used at ceremonies to offer sacrifices to the gods of heaven and earth. There are several groups of human figures with flat-topped caps.

3. 玉锄。白色，似舌形，中有圆孔，为穿柄之处。长20.5公分。

A jade hoe, white, 20.5cm long. It is tongue-shaped with a round hole in the center for the handle.

86 三星堆 SANXINGDUI

1. 各种玉璋。
   Various jade tablets.
2. 玉戚。呈白色，身扁平，两侧刻有五齿，戚是古代兵器的一种。这个玉戚显然不是作为实用器，而是作礼器使用。
   Qi was an ancient weapon. The one in the picture made of a piece of white, flat jade with five teeth on the sides was used as a sacrificial vessel.

化土成器

THE CHARM OF POTTERY FROM THE ANCIENT TOWN,
AN ART OF TURNING CLAY INTO OBJECTS

古城陶韵

各种陶盉。多为泥制灰陶，顶部隆起，下有三圆锥状足，中空，多为温酒用。
Various kinds of *he* made of gray clay with a protuberating top and three cone-shaped legs and a hollow body. *He* was a wine-drinking vessel in ancient times.

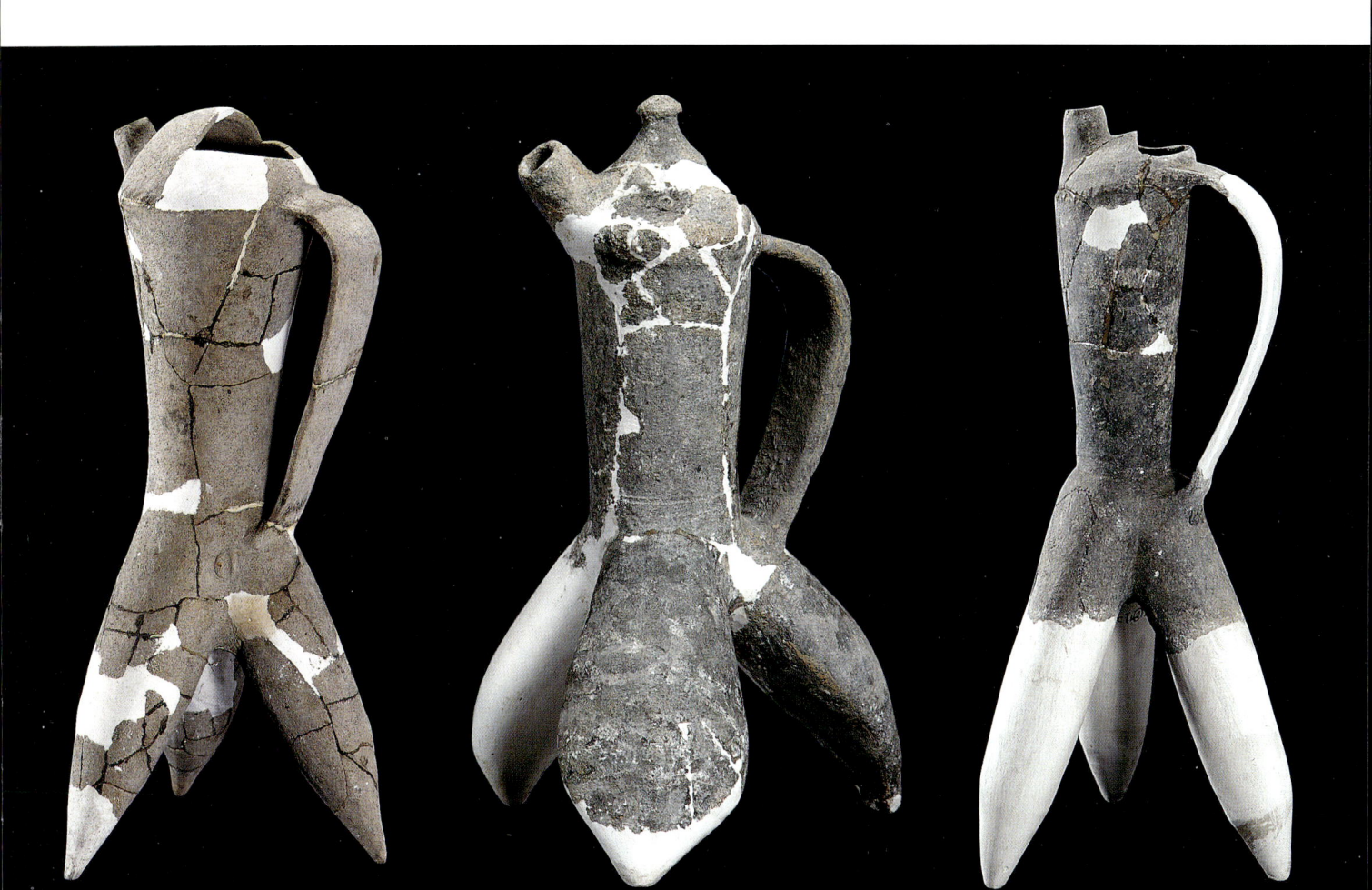

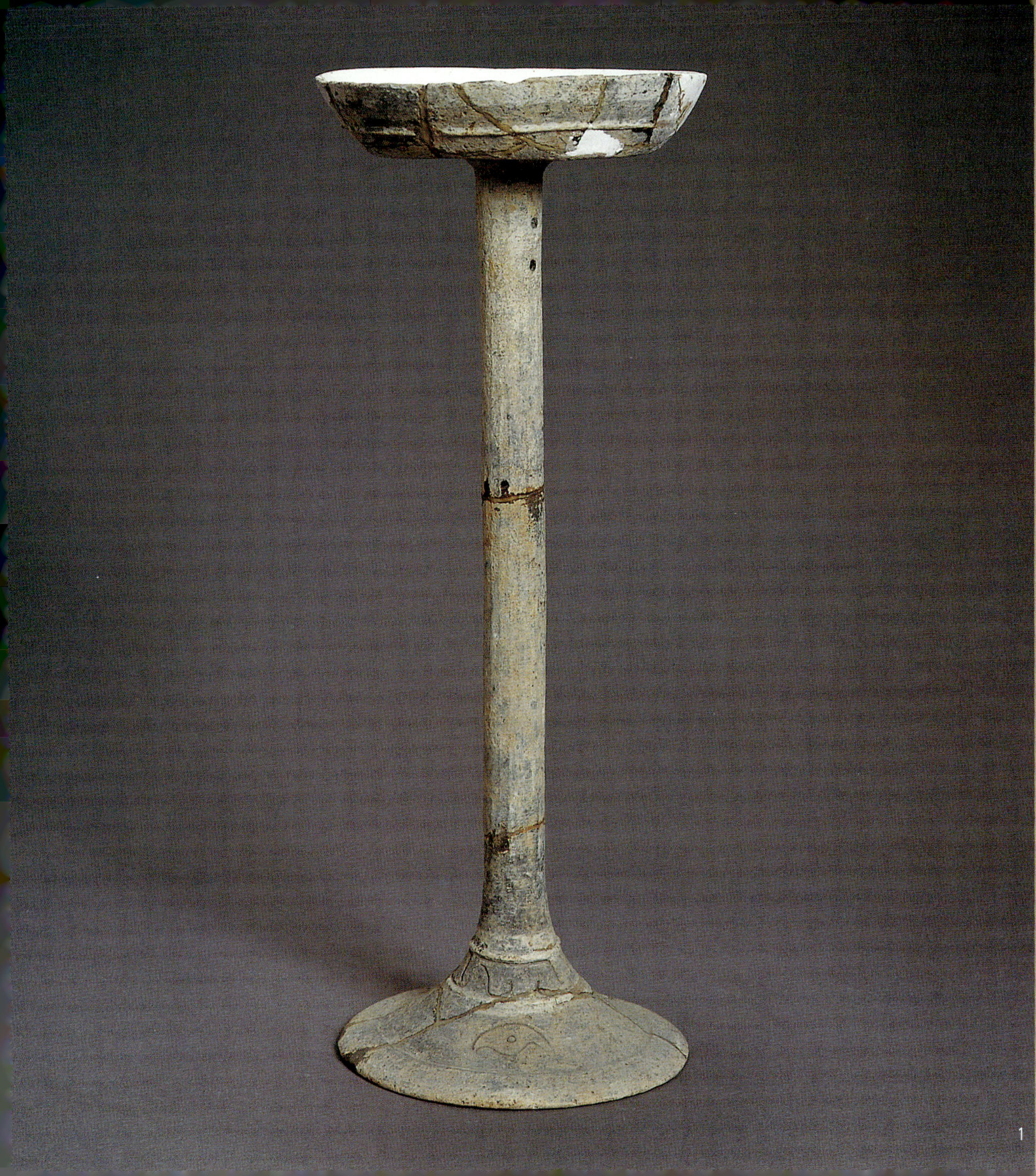

1

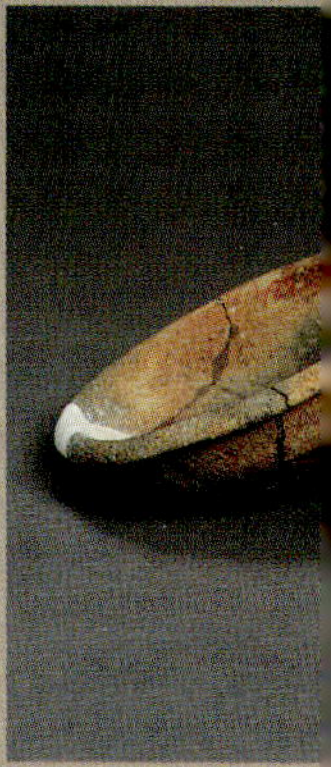

1. 陶高柄豆。一种盛物器皿。
   Dou, a high-stemmed pottery cup in ancient times.
2,3. 陶盆、陶罐。
   Pottery basins and jars.

陶三足炊器。高 39.9 公分。
A three-legged pottery cooking vessel, 39.9cm high.

三星堆 SANXINGDUI 93

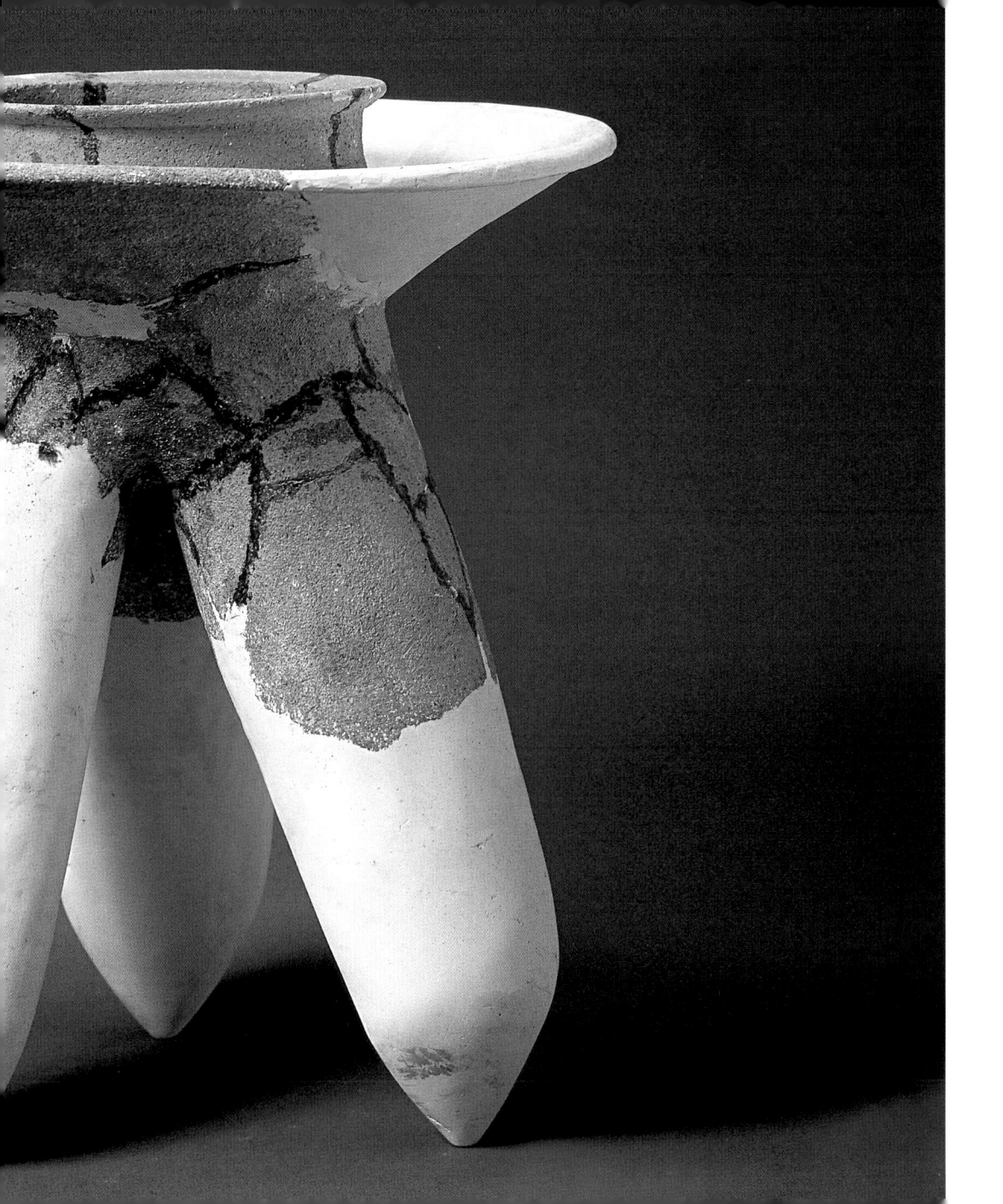

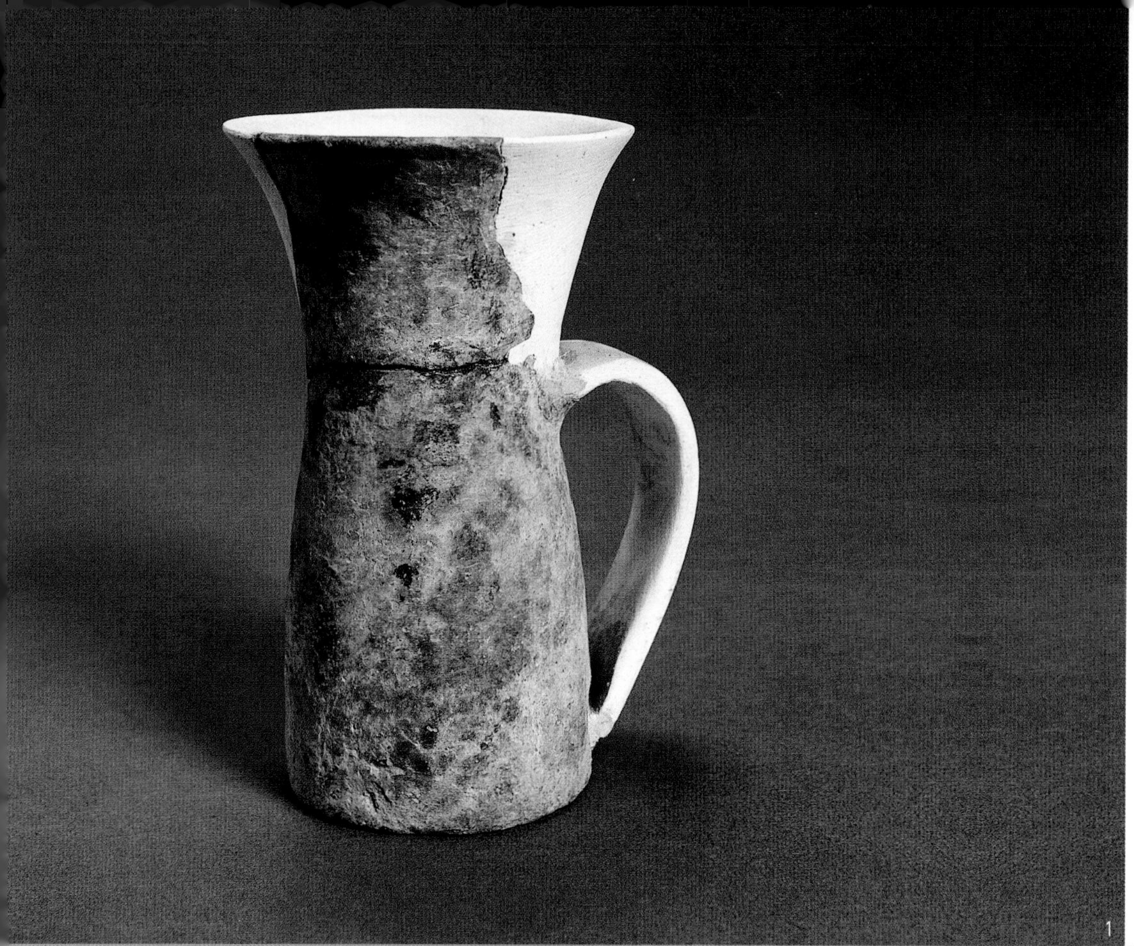

1

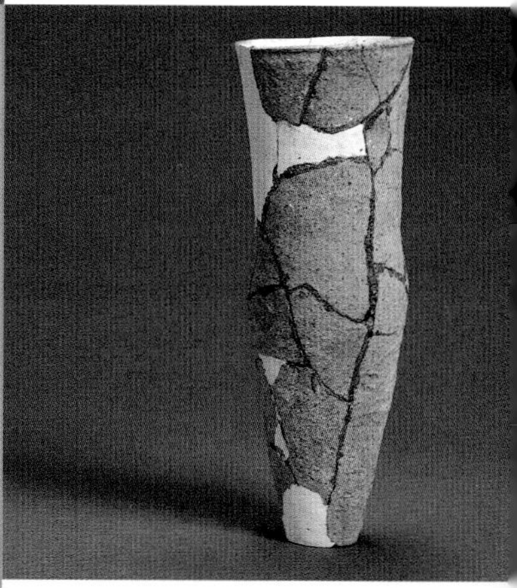

各种平底罐、高领罐、瓶形杯。造型已渗入多种外来文化因素。
Various jars with a flat bottom or a long neck and bottle-shaped cups. Their shapes show the influence of foreign culture.

主　　编：肖潜辉
副 主 编：刘家胜　包育智
责任编辑：陈东林
中文撰稿：范云兴
英文翻译：祝承耀
绘　　图：林　毅
装帧设计：王　昀　栾卫江　李玉芹
摄　　影：江　聪

图书在版编目(CIP)数据

古蜀文化三星堆／江聪等摄；中国旅游出版社编．
北京：中国旅游出版社，2001.7
ISBN 7-5032-1865-7

Ⅰ.古… Ⅱ.①江…②中… Ⅲ.出土文物－四川省－图录 Ⅳ.K873.71

中国版本图书馆 CIP 数据核字(2001) 第 037369 号

《古蜀文化三星堆》

出版发行：中国旅游出版社
地　　址：北京建国门内大街甲九号
邮　　编：100005
制　　版：北京利丰雅高电分制版有限公司
承　　印：北京文高印刷有限公司
版　　次：2001年7月第1版
印　　次：2001年7月第1版　第1次印刷
开　　本：850×1168毫米　1/24
印　　张：4　　005800
印　　数：1-5000册

(版权所有·翻版必究)